In My Skin I Win

Set In Soul

© 2020 Tatiana Media LLC in partnership with Set In Soul LLC

ISBN #: 978-1-949874-84-6

Published by Tatiana Media LLC

All rights reserved. No part of this journal/publication may be reproduced, stored in a retrieval system, or transmitted in any form or by any means, electronic, mechanical, photocopying, recording, scanning, or otherwise, except as permitted under Section 107 or 108 of the 1976 United States Copyright Act whatsoever without express written permission from the author, except in the case of brief quotations embodied in critical articles and reviews. Please refer all pertinent questions to the publisher.

Limit of Liability/Disclaimer of Warranty: While the publisher and author have used their best efforts in preparing this book/journal, they make no representations or warranties with respect to the accuracy or completeness of the contents of this book/journal and specifically disclaim any implied warranties. The advice and strategies contained herein may not be suitable for your situation. You should consult with a professional where appropriate. Neither the publisher nor author shall be liable for any loss of profit or any other emotional, physical, spiritual and mental distress and damages, including but not limited to special, incidental, consequential, or other damages.

For general information on our other products and services, please contact our Customer Support within the United States at support@setinsoul.com.

Tatiana Media LLC as well as Set In Soul LLC publishes its books in a variety of electronic formats. Some content that appears in print may not be available in electronic books.

This Journal Belongs To

Dedicated To Me Being Accepted By Me

Table Of Contents

My Experiences	8
Thoughts Towards My Ethnicity And Race	12
How I Truly Feel	21
Loving Me For Who I Am	55

How To Use This Journal

When it comes to family and friends, we are taught to believe that these groups of people are who we are to feel most comfortable around in terms of being 'ourselves.' Even when it comes to your own racial group, you may believe that this is the group where you can 'be you.' But this is not always the case for everyone. You may have heard derogatory comments towards the complexion of your skin, pattern of your hair, facial features or even personality by people within your family, group of friends or by individuals who you would least expect it from. You may find that lighter skinned or darker skinned individuals are being given preferential treatment within your family and/or society simply because of their appearance. While these individuals may seem to be favored and accepted because they are closer to society's idea of beauty and/or have the 'right' personality to match their racial group, you must remember that you are just as important, good looking, amazing and favored by the right people for who you are.

Being judged based off of your skin color, race, ethnicity, hair pattern, personality and other facial/body features is an act by those who may not know any better and/or are simply trying to deflect their insecurities on towards you. You are not alone in experiencing this. As cruel as it is, the truth is this happens every day to many people. But what if the tables were turned? What are the effects of you placing negative thoughts and judgements towards yourself because you believe you do not fit into society's idea of the 'cool and gorgeous' individual that is being portrayed? How do you overcome the criticism you've placed on yourself and come to a place of acceptance and love while also being able to exude that love towards others? What do you do when it's individuals who look just like you judging you and telling you negative things because you do not look like the world's standard of beauty? It is time to release the thought that you must 'fit in' to live the life you want and embrace the thought that you were designed by no mistake. Every detail that naturally makes up the beauty of you is to be loved, nurtured and cherished. Not everyone will understand it, but the history in your features are to be adored.

This journal addresses colorism and overall self-acceptance of facial/body features, personality and race/ethnicity. It is here you will get to the root of your feelings and rebuild with a mind frame that more than just 'accepts' who you are but loves everything ancestral and beyond that makes you you. This journal is here to be your quiet but impactful best friend. What does this mean? This means letting it all out….the parts that you love, hate, want to change and more about yourself. By using this journal you will also decimate the idea that you must act and/or be a certain way to be accepted. You will start to celebrate everything that they (those who've made their hurtful comments) say about you that is 'too big' or 'too small' or just 'not enough' or even 'too much' as being just right for you.

This journal should be filled out every morning to set the tone for how you view yourself each day. There are daily love affirmations that should be repeated to yourself each day throughout the day to help build and/or strengthen positive thoughts and beliefs about yourself. The motivational quotes sprinkled throughout this journal are there to simply remind you of the incredible person you are despite how different you may be to others. By fully embracing every part of you (the parts that you and other people are taught to dislike), we encourage you to feel love and win in the skin you are in. Let's get started.

My Experiences

My Experiences With People Within My Race And Outside Of My Race Towards My Hair....

My Experiences With People Within My Race And Outside Of My Race Towards My Skin Complexion....

My Experiences With People Within My Race And Outside Of My Race Towards The Way I Talk/Act And/Or Things I Have An Interest In....

Thoughts Towards My Ethnicity And Race

Thoughts Towards My Ethnicity And Race

What Is My Ethnicity?

Do I Love My Ethnicity And My Heritage?

My Identity Is Made Up Of:

Do I Like My Last Name?

My Last Name Represents:

Thoughts Towards My Ethnicity And Race

In What Ways Have I Altered My Facial Features To Look 'Better' (Answer If Applicable)?

What Is 'Better' To Me (Based On My Response To The Previous Prompt - Answer If Applicable)?

Why Is This Considered 'Better' To Me (Based On My Response To The Previous Prompt)?

What Other Languages Do I Know?

How Do I Distance Myself From My Native Language (Answer If Applicable)?

Thoughts Towards My Ethnicity And Race

When I Hear People With Accents Like Mine (Answer If Applicable):

I Try To Keep My Distance From:

I Look Down On:

I Have Looked Down On:

I Do Not Want To:

Thoughts Towards My Ethnicity And Race

What Do I Believe Is Keeping Me From Reaching My Full Potential?

When I See My Family, I See:

I Fantasize:

I Will Stop Appeasing:

I Want Acceptance From:

Thoughts Towards My Ethnicity And Race

I Am Ashamed Of:

Why Do I Feel Ashamed (Based On My Previous Response)?

I Get Embarrassed When:

Why Do I Feel Embarrassed (Based On My Previous Response)?

Amazing People I Admire Who Have Accomplished Wonderful Things Who I Share The Same Ethnicity And/Or Race With:

Thoughts Towards My Ethnicity And Race

When People Tease Me About My Ethnicity And/Or Race, They Say:

When People Tease Me About My Ethnicity And/Or Race, I Feel:

When People Tease Me About My Ethnicity And/Or Race, I Respond:

It Bothers Me When People Say Anything Negative About My Ethnicity And/Or Race Because:

Do I Believe The People Making Negative Comments About My Ethnicity And/Or Race Have A 'Better' Ethnicity And/Or Race Than Me?

Thoughts Towards My Ethnicity And Race

If The Answer Is Yes To The Previous Prompt, Why Do I Believe That?

I Want People To View My Ethnicity And/Or Race:

I Am Proud To Be:

I Am Not Proud To Be:

People Within My Ethnicity Have These Similar Features:

Thoughts Towards My Ethnicity And Race

Sterotypes About My Ethnicity And/Or Race:

Great Things About My Ethnicity And/Or Race:

I Am _____ Because Of My Ethnicity.

How I Truly Feel

How I Truly Feel

What Is Colorism?

My Hair Is:

My Skin Is:

I Look:

My Body Is:

How I Truly Feel

What Have People Said About My Lips/Nose/Butt/Eyelids (Answer If Applicable)?

When I Look At Myself, I See:

I Wish I Was:

Based On The Response I Gave To The Previous Prompt, Why?

When I Touch My Hair:

How I Truly Feel

When Others See Me, I Believe They See:

I Treat Lighter Skin People:

I Treat Darker Skin People:

I Believe Darker Skin Is:

I Believe Lighter Skin Is:

How I Truly Feel

The Types Of People That I Think Are Beautiful:

My Mother's Skin And Hair:

My Mother Faced:

My Father's Skin And Hair:

My Father Faced:

How I Truly Feel

My Grandmother's Skin And Hair:

My Grandmother Faced:

My Grandfather's Skin And Hair:

My Grandfather Faced:

I Do Not Want To Be:

How I Truly Feel

I Want To Be:

I Believe Skin Color Is:

I Believe Lighter Skin People Have The Advantage Of:

I Believe Darker Skin People Have The Advantage Of:

I Believe Lighter Skin People Have The Disadvantage Of:

How I Truly Feel

I Believe Darker Skin People Have The Disadvantage Of:

I Believe I Am Light Skin Because (Answer If Applicable):

I Believe I Am Dark Skin Because (Answer If Applicable):

I Believe You Are Unattractive If:

I Feel Desirable When:

How I Truly Feel

My Skin And Hair Color Represents:

Do I Believe Skin Color Plays A Role In The Concept Of Mainstream Beauty?

Do I Consider Myself Good Looking?

Struggles I Have Had Growing Up Dark Skin (Answer If Applicable):

Struggles I Have Had Growing Up Light Skin (Answer If Applicable):

How I Truly Feel

I Dislike My Complexion Because:

I Love My Complexion Because:

I View Lighter Skin Individuals:

I Believe Lighter Skin People:

I Noticed Lighter Skin People:

How I Truly Feel

I View Darker Skin Individuals:

I Believe Darker Skin People:

I Noticed Darker Skin People:

I Have Been Made To Feel _____ In My Skin.

Because I Have The Darkest Skin In My Family (Answer If Applicable):

How I Truly Feel

Because I Have The Lightest Skin In My Family (Answer If Applicable):

I Believe I Have Been Conditioned To Believe:

Why Do I Believe What I Responded To From The Previous Prompt?

I Have Heard Family Members Say:

I Believe I Wasn't Pretty/Handsome Because (Answer If Applicable):

I Believe I Would Look Better:

I Dislike Hearing:

What Have I Done To Get My Skin The Complexion I Wanted (Answer If Applicable)?

Do I Look Better When I Tried To Get The Skin Complexion Desired (Answer If Applicable)?

I Am Different (List In What Ways):

How I Truly Feel

Feelings Of Disgust I Have Had Towards Myself In Regards To My Skin Color (Answer If Applicable):

I Believe My Facial Features Are:

I Do Not Feel 'Good Enough' Because:

My Eye Color Is:

My Eye Shape Is:

How I Truly Feel

My Nose Is:

My Lips Are:

My Face Is Shaped:

What Do I Consider An Exotic Look?

People Treat Me:

How I Truly Feel

Why Do I Believe People Treat Me The Way I Answered In The Previous Prompt?

When I _____, People Treat Me:

I Believe Others Are Well Liked Over Me Because (Answer If Applicable):

I Have Been Bullied For (Answer If Applicable):

I Have Bullied Others For (Answer If Applicable):

How I Truly Feel

It Hurts Me When:

I Want To Change _____ Because:

I Always Want To Prove:

If No One Teased Me, Would I Still Want To Change Anything (Answer If Applicable)?

If The Answer Is Yes To The Previous Prompt, Why Do I Still Want This Change?

How I Truly Feel

How Far Would I Be Willing To Go To Change My Appearance And Personality To Fit In?

What Types Of People Make Fun Of Me (Answer If Applicable)?

Would I Want To Be Like Or Look Like The People Who Have Teased Me (Answer If Applicable)?

What Parts Of Me Do/Have People Tease Me About?

My Hair Will Not:

How I Truly Feel

My Hair Will:

I Believe God Made Me Like This Because:

I Believe Beauty Is:

I Am Unique Because:

I Look Different Because:

How I Truly Feel

My Curls (Answer If Applicable):

Have I Ever Teased Anyone For Their Looks?

If I Answered Yes To The Previous Prompt, Who Have I Teased For Their Looks And Why?

I Believe Life Would Be Easier For Me If:

No One Teases:

People Tease Me Because (Answer If Applicable):

Negative Comments I Have Received:

Positive Comments I Have Received:

I Can Tell When:

My Own Racial Group Discriminates Against Me By:

I Felt Humiliated When:

Have I Been Punished/Reprimanded For Wearing Certain Natural Hairstyles When I Wear My Natural Hair Texture?

If I Changed My Looks, Would My Attitude Change?

Would I Want To Be Friends With The People Who Won't Accept A Person Like Me?

Based On The Response I Gave In The Previous Prompt, Why Or Why Not?

How I Truly Feel

Colors That Look Good On Me:

Based On My Answer To The Previous Prompt, Why Do I Believe These Colors Look Good On Me?

If I Were To Change Anything, I Would Want To Achieve A Change In (Answer If Applicable):

I Just Want To Be:

Being Confident Means:

How I Truly Feel

People Who Look Like Me That I Believe Are Beautiful/Handsome:

I Will Not Be Insecure About:

I Am Choosing To Love:

I Will Not Stop Loving:

I Feel Loved When:

How I Truly Feel

My Skin Feels:

My Skin Is Special Because:

With Love And Care, My Skin And Hair:

The People Who Speak Negativity Towards Me And My Skin Complexion Are Experiencing:

I Know My Beauty:

How I Truly Feel

My Skin Is Beautiful Because:

People Who Judge Me About My Skin:

I Am Deserving Of:

I Am More Than:

I Am Not Less Than:

How I Truly Feel

Who Do I Resemble Within My Family?

To Be Accepted, Society Has Told Me I Must:

I Will Not Change:

I Am Learning That I Could Never Be:

I Am Accepting:

How I Truly Feel

Having Freckles (Answer If Applicable):

Being Albino (Answer If Applicable):

My Skin Has Protected Me From:

I Tan To Become (Answer If Appliable):

I Bleach To Become (Answer If Applicable):

How I Truly Feel

I Believe God Gave Me My Skin Complexion:

Before I Did Not Love My Skin, But Now:

Things I Use To Do To My Skin (Answer If Applicable):

What I Love About Doing My Hair:

My Hair Loves:

My Hair Feels Great With:

I Take Care Of My Hair By:

What Is 'Good Hair'?

What Does Society Consider 'Good Hair'?

What Do I Consider To Be 'Good Hair'?

What Is 'Not Good Hair'?

What Does Society Consider 'Not Good Hair'?

What Do I Consider To Be 'Not Good Hair'?

My Hair Is 'Good Hair' Because:

What I Am Learning To Love About My Hair:

How I Truly Feel

My Hair Deserves:

Ways I Show Love To My Hair:

I Am Learning That My Hair:

Evolving With My Hair/Hairstyles Feels:

My Hair Thrives:

How I Truly Feel

I Will Not Alter:

Things I Like To Do That A Majority Of Others That Look Like Me Do Not Like To Do:

Things I Like To Eat That A Majority Of Others That Look Like Me Do Not Like To Eat:

Things I Do Not Like To Eat That A Majority Of People Who Look Like Me Love To Eat:

I Am Considered _____ Because I Like

_____.

How I Truly Feel

I Am Considered _____

Because I Do Not _____.

People Around Me Say When I Speak I Sound _____

_____.

People Around Me Say I Act _____

_____.

Being Myself Means _____

_____.

Loving Me For Who I Am

Loving Me For Who I Am

Date: Mood:

What I Love About My Hair Today: I Will Not Allow Others Who Look Like Me To Tell Me:

What I Love About My Skin Today: I Will Not Allow Others Who Do Not Look Like Me To Tell Me:

I Am Proud To Be: It Is Okay If I Am The Only One:

I Am Beautiful/Good Looking Because: It Is Okay If I Do Not Fit Into:

The Last Negative Comment I Received Towards My Appearance/Personality And My Thoughts Towards The Comment: Everyday I Am Learning To Accept:

How Did I Respond Towards The Comment Made In The Previous Prompt?   Just Because I Don't/Do

_____, Doesn't Mean I:

It Is Okay For Me To Like

_____

And Still Be:

I Know That I Am Unique And Beautiful In Every Special Way.

Loving Me For Who I Am

Date: Mood:

What I Love About My Hair Today: | I Will Not Allow Others Who Look Like Me To Tell Me:

What I Love About My Skin Today: | I Will Not Allow Others Who Do Not Look Like Me To Tell Me:

I Am Proud To Be: | It Is Okay If I Am The Only One:

I Am Beautiful/Good Looking Because: | It Is Okay If I Do Not Fit Into:

The Last Negative Comment I Received Towards My Appearance/Personality And My Thoughts Towards The Comment: | Everyday I Am Learning To Accept:

How Did I Respond Towards The Comment Made In The Previous Prompt? | Just Because I Don't/Do

_____, Doesn't Mean I:

It Is Okay For Me To Like

_____

And Still Be:

Loving Me For Who I Am

Date: Mood:

What I Love About My Hair Today: I Will Not Allow Others Who Look Like Me To Tell Me:

What I Love About My Skin Today: I Will Not Allow Others Who Do Not Look Like Me To Tell Me:

I Am Proud To Be: It Is Okay If I Am The Only One:

I Am Beautiful/Good Looking Because: It Is Okay If I Do Not Fit Into:

The Last Negative Comment I Received Towards My Appearance/Personality And My Thoughts Towards The Comment: Everyday I Am Learning To Accept:

How Did I Respond Towards The Comment Made In The Previous Prompt?   Just Because I Don't/Do

_____, Doesn't Mean I:

It Is Okay For Me To Like

_____

And Still Be:

Every Person Deserves Love And Happiness Regardless Of Their Skin Color, And That Includes Me.

My Hair Is Beautiful As It Is.

My Complexion Is Perfect.

Loving Me For Who I Am

Date: Mood:

What I Love About My Hair Today: | I Will Not Allow Others Who Look Like Me To Tell Me:

What I Love About My Skin Today: | I Will Not Allow Others Who Do Not Look Like Me To Tell Me:

I Am Proud To Be: | It Is Okay If I Am The Only One:

I Am Beautiful/Good Looking Because: | It Is Okay If I Do Not Fit Into:

The Last Negative Comment I Received Towards My Appearance/Personality And My Thoughts Towards The Comment: | Everyday I Am Learning To Accept:

How Did I Respond Towards The Comment Made In The Previous Prompt? | Just Because I Don't/Do

_____, Doesn't Mean I:

It Is Okay For Me To Like

_____

And Still Be:

Loving Me For Who I Am

Date:	Mood:

What I Love About My Hair Today:

I Will Not Allow Others Who Look Like Me To Tell Me:

What I Love About My Skin Today:

I Will Not Allow Others Who Do Not Look Like Me To Tell Me:

I Am Proud To Be:

It Is Okay If I Am The Only One:

I Am Beautiful/Good Looking Because:

It Is Okay If I Do Not Fit Into:

The Last Negative Comment I Received Towards My Appearance/Personality And My Thoughts Towards The Comment:

Everyday I Am Learning To Accept:

How Did I Respond Towards The Comment Made In The Previous Prompt?

Just Because I Don't/Do

_____, Doesn't Mean I:

It Is Okay For Me To Like

_____

And Still Be:

Loving Me For Who I Am

Date: Mood:

What I Love About My Hair Today: I Will Not Allow Others Who Look Like Me To Tell Me:

What I Love About My Skin Today: I Will Not Allow Others Who Do Not Look Like Me To Tell Me:

I Am Proud To Be: It Is Okay If I Am The Only One:

I Am Beautiful/Good Looking Because: It Is Okay If I Do Not Fit Into:

The Last Negative Comment I Received Towards My Appearance/Personality And My Thoughts Towards The Comment: Everyday I Am Learning To Accept:

How Did I Respond Towards The Comment Made In The Previous Prompt?   Just Because I Don't/Do

_____, Doesn't Mean I:

It Is Okay For Me To Like
_____
And Still Be:

It May Take Some Time But I Am Overcoming My Insecurities.

Ways I Build My Self Esteem Up....

My Thoughts

Loving Me For Who I Am

Date: Mood:

What I Love About My Hair Today: I Will Not Allow Others Who Look Like Me To Tell Me:

What I Love About My Skin Today: I Will Not Allow Others Who Do Not Look Like Me To Tell Me:

I Am Proud To Be: It Is Okay If I Am The Only One:

I Am Beautiful/Good Looking Because: It Is Okay If I Do Not Fit Into:

The Last Negative Comment I Received Towards My Appearance/Personality And My Thoughts Towards The Comment: Everyday I Am Learning To Accept:

How Did I Respond Towards The Comment Made In The Previous Prompt?   Just Because I Don't/Do

_____, Doesn't Mean I:

It Is Okay For Me To Like

_____

And Still Be:

There Is Beauty In Every Person, Every Race, And Every Shade.

Loving Me For Who I Am

Date: Mood:

What I Love About My Hair Today: I Will Not Allow Others Who Look Like Me To Tell Me:

What I Love About My Skin Today: I Will Not Allow Others Who Do Not Look Like Me To Tell Me:

I Am Proud To Be: It Is Okay If I Am The Only One:

I Am Beautiful/Good Looking Because: It Is Okay If I Do Not Fit Into:

The Last Negative Comment I Received Towards My Appearance/Personality And My Thoughts Towards The Comment: Everyday I Am Learning To Accept:

How Did I Respond Towards The Comment Made In The Previous Prompt?   Just Because I Don't/Do

_____, Doesn't Mean I:

It Is Okay For Me To Like
_____
And Still Be:

I Am Proud Of My Skin Color And Distinct Facial Features.

God Blessed Me With A Beautiful Voice.

Loving Me For Who I Am

Date: Mood:

What I Love About My Hair Today: | I Will Not Allow Others Who Look Like Me To Tell Me:

What I Love About My Skin Today: | I Will Not Allow Others Who Do Not Look Like Me To Tell Me:

I Am Proud To Be: | It Is Okay If I Am The Only One:

I Am Beautiful/Good Looking Because: | It Is Okay If I Do Not Fit Into:

The Last Negative Comment I Received Towards My Appearance/Personality And My Thoughts Towards The Comment: | Everyday I Am Learning To Accept:

How Did I Respond Towards The Comment Made In The Previous Prompt? | Just Because I Don't/Do

_____, Doesn't Mean I:

It Is Okay For Me To Like

_____

And Still Be:

Names People Call Me....

Names I Call Myself....

My Thoughts

Loving Me For Who I Am

Date: Mood:

What I Love About My Hair Today: I Will Not Allow Others Who Look Like Me To Tell Me:

What I Love About My Skin Today: I Will Not Allow Others Who Do Not Look Like Me To Tell Me:

I Am Proud To Be: It Is Okay If I Am The Only One:

I Am Beautiful/Good Looking Because: It Is Okay If I Do Not Fit Into:

The Last Negative Comment I Received Towards My Appearance/Personality And My Thoughts Towards The Comment: Everyday I Am Learning To Accept:

How Did I Respond Towards The Comment Made In The Previous Prompt?   Just Because I Don't/Do

_____, Doesn't Mean I:

It Is Okay For Me To Like

_____

And Still Be:

I See Opportunities For A Better And More Diverse World Wherever I Go.

Loving Me For Who I Am

Date: Mood:

What I Love About My Hair Today: I Will Not Allow Others Who Look Like Me To Tell Me:

What I Love About My Skin Today: I Will Not Allow Others Who Do Not Look Like Me To Tell Me:

I Am Proud To Be: It Is Okay If I Am The Only One:

I Am Beautiful/Good Looking Because: It Is Okay If I Do Not Fit Into:

The Last Negative Comment I Received Towards My Appearance/Personality And My Thoughts Towards The Comment: Everyday I Am Learning To Accept:

How Did I Respond Towards The Comment Made In The Previous Prompt?   Just Because I Don't/Do

_____, Doesn't Mean I:

It Is Okay For Me To Like
_____
And Still Be:

I Am Proud Of My History And Encourage Others To Discover The Beauty Of What I Represent.

73

The Way I Talk And The Way I Dress Are The Parts That Make Me Me.

Loving Me For Who I Am

Date: Mood:

What I Love About My Hair Today: | I Will Not Allow Others Who Look Like Me To Tell Me:

What I Love About My Skin Today: | I Will Not Allow Others Who Do Not Look Like Me To Tell Me:

I Am Proud To Be: | It Is Okay If I Am The Only One:

I Am Beautiful/Good Looking Because: | It Is Okay If I Do Not Fit Into:

The Last Negative Comment I Received Towards My Appearance/Personality And My Thoughts Towards The Comment: | Everyday I Am Learning To Accept:

How Did I Respond Towards The Comment Made In The Previous Prompt? | Just Because I Don't/Do

_____, Doesn't Mean I:

It Is Okay For Me To Like

_____

And Still Be:

I Try To Stay Away From....

Loving Me For Who I Am

Date: Mood:

What I Love About My Hair Today: I Will Not Allow Others Who Look Like Me To Tell Me:

What I Love About My Skin Today: I Will Not Allow Others Who Do Not Look Like Me To Tell Me:

I Am Proud To Be: It Is Okay If I Am The Only One:

I Am Beautiful/Good Looking Because: It Is Okay If I Do Not Fit Into:

The Last Negative Comment I Received Towards My Appearance/Personality And My Thoughts Towards The Comment: Everyday I Am Learning To Accept:

How Did I Respond Towards The Comment Made In The Previous Prompt?   Just Because I Don't/Do

_____, Doesn't Mean I:

It Is Okay For Me To Like
_____
And Still Be:

My Features Are Unique And Make Me Stand Out, Which Is Way Better Than Being Invisible.

Loving Me For Who I Am

Date: Mood:

What I Love About My Hair Today: I Will Not Allow Others Who Look Like Me To Tell Me:

What I Love About My Skin Today: I Will Not Allow Others Who Do Not Look Like Me To Tell Me:

I Am Proud To Be: It Is Okay If I Am The Only One:

I Am Beautiful/Good Looking Because: It Is Okay If I Do Not Fit Into:

The Last Negative Comment I Received Towards My Appearance/Personality And My Thoughts Towards The Comment: Everyday I Am Learning To Accept:

How Did I Respond Towards The Comment Made In The Previous Prompt?   Just Because I Don't/Do

_____, Doesn't Mean I:

It Is Okay For Me To Like

_____

And Still Be:

My Thoughts

Loving Me For Who I Am

Date: Mood:

What I Love About My Hair Today: I Will Not Allow Others Who Look Like Me To Tell Me:

What I Love About My Skin Today: I Will Not Allow Others Who Do Not Look Like Me To Tell Me:

I Am Proud To Be: It Is Okay If I Am The Only One:

I Am Beautiful/Good Looking Because: It Is Okay If I Do Not Fit Into:

The Last Negative Comment I Received Towards My Appearance/Personality And My Thoughts Towards The Comment: Everyday I Am Learning To Accept:

How Did I Respond Towards The Comment Made In The Previous Prompt?   Just Because I Don't/Do
_____, Doesn't Mean I:

It Is Okay For Me To Like
_____
And Still Be:

You Can See My Beauty Inside And Out.

What Makes Me Different Is What Makes Me Stand Out And Shine.

No Matter What Others Think, Their Opinions No Longer Have An Impact On Me.

Loving Me For Who I Am

Date: Mood:

What I Love About My Hair Today: I Will Not Allow Others Who Look Like Me To Tell Me:

What I Love About My Skin Today: I Will Not Allow Others Who Do Not Look Like Me To Tell Me:

I Am Proud To Be: It Is Okay If I Am The Only One:

I Am Beautiful/Good Looking Because: It Is Okay If I Do Not Fit Into:

The Last Negative Comment I Received Towards My Appearance/Personality And My Thoughts Towards The Comment: Everyday I Am Learning To Accept:

How Did I Respond Towards The Comment Made In The Previous Prompt?   Just Because I Don't/Do

_____, Doesn't Mean I:

It Is Okay For Me To Like

_____

And Still Be:

Many People Admire How I Look — I Am Different And Exotic And Beautiful.

83

Loving Me For Who I Am

Date: Mood:

What I Love About My Hair Today: I Will Not Allow Others Who Look Like Me To Tell Me:

What I Love About My Skin Today: I Will Not Allow Others Who Do Not Look Like Me To Tell Me:

I Am Proud To Be: It Is Okay If I Am The Only One:

I Am Beautiful/Good Looking Because: It Is Okay If I Do Not Fit Into:

The Last Negative Comment I Received Towards My Appearance/Personality And My Thoughts Towards The Comment: Everyday I Am Learning To Accept:

How Did I Respond Towards The Comment Made In The Previous Prompt?   Just Because I Don't/Do _____, Doesn't Mean I:

It Is Okay For Me To Like _____ And Still Be:

I Know How To Highlight My Best Features — And I Am Not Afraid To Flaunt 'Em! I Am Confident In My Beauty, In The Way I Look, And In The Way I Speak.

Loving Me For Who I Am

Date: Mood:

What I Love About My Hair Today: | I Will Not Allow Others Who Look Like Me To Tell Me:

What I Love About My Skin Today: | I Will Not Allow Others Who Do Not Look Like Me To Tell Me:

I Am Proud To Be: | It Is Okay If I Am The Only One:

I Am Beautiful/Good Looking Because: | It Is Okay If I Do Not Fit Into:

The Last Negative Comment I Received Towards My Appearance/Personality And My Thoughts Towards The Comment: | Everyday I Am Learning To Accept:

How Did I Respond Towards The Comment Made In The Previous Prompt? | Just Because I Don't/Do

_____, Doesn't Mean I:

It Is Okay For Me To Like

_____

And Still Be:

I Like Being Different. I Like Being Special. I Like Being Unique. I Like Who I Am.

I Am Now Embracing....

Dark Is Divine.

Loving Me For Who I Am

Date: Mood:

What I Love About My Hair Today: | I Will Not Allow Others Who Look Like Me To Tell Me:

What I Love About My Skin Today: | I Will Not Allow Others Who Do Not Look Like Me To Tell Me:

I Am Proud To Be: | It Is Okay If I Am The Only One:

I Am Beautiful/Good Looking Because: | It Is Okay If I Do Not Fit Into:

The Last Negative Comment I Received Towards My Appearance/Personality And My Thoughts Towards The Comment: | Everyday I Am Learning To Accept:

How Did I Respond Towards The Comment Made In The Previous Prompt? | Just Because I Don't/Do _____, Doesn't Mean I:

It Is Okay For Me To Like _____

And Still Be:

I View Everyone Equally, Regardless Of Their Status In Life And/Or How They Look.

88

Loving Me For Who I Am

Date: Mood:

What I Love About My Hair Today:	I Will Not Allow Others Who Look Like Me To Tell Me:
What I Love About My Skin Today:	I Will Not Allow Others Who Do Not Look Like Me To Tell Me:
I Am Proud To Be:	It Is Okay If I Am The Only One:
I Am Beautiful/Good Looking Because:	It Is Okay If I Do Not Fit Into:
The Last Negative Comment I Received Towards My Appearance/Personality And My Thoughts Towards The Comment:	Everyday I Am Learning To Accept:
How Did I Respond Towards The Comment Made In The Previous Prompt?	Just Because I Don't/Do _____, Doesn't Mean I:
It Is Okay For Me To Like _____ And Still Be:	

Loving Me For Who I Am

Date: Mood:

What I Love About My Hair Today: I Will Not Allow Others Who Look Like Me To Tell Me:

What I Love About My Skin Today: I Will Not Allow Others Who Do Not Look Like Me To Tell Me:

I Am Proud To Be: It Is Okay If I Am The Only One:

I Am Beautiful/Good Looking Because: It Is Okay If I Do Not Fit Into:

The Last Negative Comment I Received Towards My Appearance/Personality And My Thoughts Towards The Comment: Everyday I Am Learning To Accept:

How Did I Respond Towards The Comment Made In The Previous Prompt?   Just Because I Don't/Do _____, Doesn't Mean I:

It Is Okay For Me To Like _____

And Still Be:

I Refuse To Let Pride And Prejudice Get In The Way Of Achieving My Goals.

90

My Family Comes In Many Shades And We Are All Amazing.

I Do Not Need To Do Anything To 'Fit In' To Something I Was Never Suppose To 'Fit Into.'

Loving Me For Who I Am

Date: Mood:

What I Love About My Hair Today: I Will Not Allow Others Who Look Like Me To Tell Me:

What I Love About My Skin Today: I Will Not Allow Others Who Do Not Look Like Me To Tell Me:

I Am Proud To Be: It Is Okay If I Am The Only One:

I Am Beautiful/Good Looking Because: It Is Okay If I Do Not Fit Into:

The Last Negative Comment I Received Towards My Appearance/Personality And My Thoughts Towards The Comment: Everyday I Am Learning To Accept:

How Did I Respond Towards The Comment Made In The Previous Prompt?   Just Because I Don't/Do

_____, Doesn't Mean I:

It Is Okay For Me To Like
_____
And Still Be:

No One Is Better Or Less Than Me Just Because Of How They Look.

Loving Me For Who I Am

Date: Mood:

What I Love About My Hair Today: I Will Not Allow Others Who Look Like Me To Tell Me:

What I Love About My Skin Today: I Will Not Allow Others Who Do Not Look Like Me To Tell Me:

I Am Proud To Be: It Is Okay If I Am The Only One:

I Am Beautiful/Good Looking Because: It Is Okay If I Do Not Fit Into:

The Last Negative Comment I Received Towards My Appearance/Personality And My Thoughts Towards The Comment: Everyday I Am Learning To Accept:

How Did I Respond Towards The Comment Made In The Previous Prompt?   Just Because I Don't/Do

_____, Doesn't Mean I:

It Is Okay For Me To Like

_____

And Still Be:

I Have Every Right To Speak Up And Be Heard, Regardless Of My Race And/Or Ethnicity.

Loving Me For Who I Am

Date: Mood:

What I Love About My Hair Today: I Will Not Allow Others Who Look Like Me To Tell Me:

What I Love About My Skin Today: I Will Not Allow Others Who Do Not Look Like Me To Tell Me:

I Am Proud To Be: It Is Okay If I Am The Only One:

I Am Beautiful/Good Looking Because: It Is Okay If I Do Not Fit Into:

The Last Negative Comment I Received Towards My Appearance/Personality And My Thoughts Towards The Comment: Everyday I Am Learning To Accept:

How Did I Respond Towards The Comment Made In The Previous Prompt?   Just Because I Don't/Do

_____, Doesn't Mean I:

It Is Okay For Me To Like

_____

And Still Be:

> I Choose To Surround Myself With People Who Treat Everyone Equally.

I Am Glad That I Am....

Loving Me For Who I Am

Date: Mood:

What I Love About My Hair Today: I Will Not Allow Others Who Look Like Me To Tell Me:

What I Love About My Skin Today: I Will Not Allow Others Who Do Not Look Like Me To Tell Me:

I Am Proud To Be: It Is Okay If I Am The Only One:

I Am Beautiful/Good Looking Because: It Is Okay If I Do Not Fit Into:

The Last Negative Comment I Received Towards My Appearance/Personality And My Thoughts Towards The Comment: Everyday I Am Learning To Accept:

How Did I Respond Towards The Comment Made In The Previous Prompt?   Just Because I Don't/Do

_____, Doesn't Mean I:

It Is Okay For Me To Like

_____

And Still Be:

I Believe That One's Real Worth Lies Within How You Treat Others And Yourself.

I Am The Definition Of Beauty.

My Thoughts

Loving Me For Who I Am

Date: Mood:

What I Love About My Hair Today: I Will Not Allow Others Who Look Like Me To Tell Me:

What I Love About My Skin Today: I Will Not Allow Others Who Do Not Look Like Me To Tell Me:

I Am Proud To Be: It Is Okay If I Am The Only One:

I Am Beautiful/Good Looking Because: It Is Okay If I Do Not Fit Into:

The Last Negative Comment I Received Towards My Appearance/Personality And My Thoughts Towards The Comment: Everyday I Am Learning To Accept:

How Did I Respond Towards The Comment Made In The Previous Prompt?   Just Because I Don't/Do

_____, Doesn't Mean I:

It Is Okay For Me To Like

_____

And Still Be:

I Believe In Meritocracy And Getting Ahead Because Of Your Achievements Instead Of How You Look.

100

Loving Me For Who I Am

Date: Mood:

What I Love About My Hair Today: | I Will Not Allow Others Who Look Like Me To Tell Me:

What I Love About My Skin Today: | I Will Not Allow Others Who Do Not Look Like Me To Tell Me:

I Am Proud To Be: | It Is Okay If I Am The Only One:

I Am Beautiful/Good Looking Because: | It Is Okay If I Do Not Fit Into:

The Last Negative Comment I Received Towards My Appearance/Personality And My Thoughts Towards The Comment: | Everyday I Am Learning To Accept:

How Did I Respond Towards The Comment Made In The Previous Prompt? | Just Because I Don't/Do

_____, Doesn't Mean I:

It Is Okay For Me To Like

_____

And Still Be:

I Am Beginning To Love Myself. Now I Am Healing.

When I Was Younger, I Was Not Allowed....

Loving Me For Who I Am

Date: Mood:

What I Love About My Hair Today: I Will Not Allow Others Who Look Like Me To Tell Me:

What I Love About My Skin Today: I Will Not Allow Others Who Do Not Look Like Me To Tell Me:

I Am Proud To Be: It Is Okay If I Am The Only One:

I Am Beautiful/Good Looking Because: It Is Okay If I Do Not Fit Into:

The Last Negative Comment I Received Towards My Appearance/Personality And My Thoughts Towards The Comment: Everyday I Am Learning To Accept:

How Did I Respond Towards The Comment Made In The Previous Prompt?   Just Because I Don't/Do

_____, Doesn't Mean I:

It Is Okay For Me To Like
_____
And Still Be:

Loving Me For Who I Am

Date: Mood:

What I Love About My Hair Today: I Will Not Allow Others Who Look Like
                                                   Me To Tell Me:

What I Love About My Skin Today: I Will Not Allow Others Who Do Not
                                                   Look Like Me To Tell Me:

I Am Proud To Be: It Is Okay If I Am The Only One:

I Am Beautiful/Good Looking   It Is Okay If I Do Not Fit Into:
Because:

The Last Negative Comment I   Everyday I Am Learning To Accept:
Received Towards My Appearance/
Personality And My Thoughts
Towards The Comment:

How Did I Respond Towards The   Just Because I Don't/Do
Comment Made In The Previous
Prompt?   _____, Doesn't Mean I:

It Is Okay For Me To Like

_____

And Still Be:

I Take Care Of Myself And My Body Because I Know That My Body Is An Instrument That Is Proudly Showcasing My Heritage To The World.

I Am Not Just Accepting Myself But I Am Also Loving Myself For Who I Am.

Loving Me For Who I Am

Date: Mood:

What I Love About My Hair Today: | I Will Not Allow Others Who Look Like Me To Tell Me:

What I Love About My Skin Today: | I Will Not Allow Others Who Do Not Look Like Me To Tell Me:

I Am Proud To Be: | It Is Okay If I Am The Only One:

I Am Beautiful/Good Looking Because: | It Is Okay If I Do Not Fit Into:

The Last Negative Comment I Received Towards My Appearance/Personality And My Thoughts Towards The Comment: | Everyday I Am Learning To Accept:

How Did I Respond Towards The Comment Made In The Previous Prompt? | Just Because I Don't/Do

_____, Doesn't Mean I:

It Is Okay For Me To Like

_____

And Still Be:

Loving Me For Who I Am

Date: Mood:

What I Love About My Hair Today: I Will Not Allow Others Who Look Like Me To Tell Me:

What I Love About My Skin Today: I Will Not Allow Others Who Do Not Look Like Me To Tell Me:

I Am Proud To Be: It Is Okay If I Am The Only One:

I Am Beautiful/Good Looking Because: It Is Okay If I Do Not Fit Into:

The Last Negative Comment I Received Towards My Appearance/Personality And My Thoughts Towards The Comment: Everyday I Am Learning To Accept:

How Did I Respond Towards The Comment Made In The Previous Prompt?   Just Because I Don't/Do

_____, Doesn't Mean I:

It Is Okay For Me To Like

_____

And Still Be:

I Judge People Based On Their Character Instead Of How Light/Dark Their Skin Is.

Loving Me For Who I Am

Date:

Mood:

What I Love About My Hair Today:

I Will Not Allow Others Who Look Like Me To Tell Me:

What I Love About My Skin Today:

I Will Not Allow Others Who Do Not Look Like Me To Tell Me:

I Am Proud To Be:

It Is Okay If I Am The Only One:

I Am Beautiful/Good Looking Because:

It Is Okay If I Do Not Fit Into:

The Last Negative Comment I Received Towards My Appearance/Personality And My Thoughts Towards The Comment:

Everyday I Am Learning To Accept:

How Did I Respond Towards The Comment Made In The Previous Prompt?

Just Because I Don't/Do

_____, Doesn't Mean I:

It Is Okay For Me To Like

_____

And Still Be:

I Am Calm When Faced With Blatant Discrimination. I Am Much Too Dignified To Stoop Down To Their Level.

My Thoughts

Loving Me For Who I Am

Date: Mood:

What I Love About My Hair Today: | I Will Not Allow Others Who Look Like Me To Tell Me:

What I Love About My Skin Today: | I Will Not Allow Others Who Do Not Look Like Me To Tell Me:

I Am Proud To Be: | It Is Okay If I Am The Only One:

I Am Beautiful/Good Looking Because: | It Is Okay If I Do Not Fit Into:

The Last Negative Comment I Received Towards My Appearance/Personality And My Thoughts Towards The Comment: | Everyday I Am Learning To Accept:

How Did I Respond Towards The Comment Made In The Previous Prompt? | Just Because I Don't/Do

_____, Doesn't Mean I:

It Is Okay For Me To Like

_____

And Still Be:

I Believe In The Golden Rule And That Is Why I Treat Everyone With Courtesy And Respect Regardless Of Their Skin Color.

Loving Me For Who I Am

Date: Mood:

What I Love About My Hair Today: I Will Not Allow Others Who Look Like Me To Tell Me:

What I Love About My Skin Today: I Will Not Allow Others Who Do Not Look Like Me To Tell Me:

I Am Proud To Be: It Is Okay If I Am The Only One:

I Am Beautiful/Good Looking Because: It Is Okay If I Do Not Fit Into:

The Last Negative Comment I Received Towards My Appearance/Personality And My Thoughts Towards The Comment: Everyday I Am Learning To Accept:

How Did I Respond Towards The Comment Made In The Previous Prompt?   Just Because I Don't/Do _____, Doesn't Mean I:

It Is Okay For Me To Like
_____
And Still Be:

I Am Beautiful And I Will Be Beautiful Forever.

Loving Me For Who I Am

Date: Mood:

What I Love About My Hair Today: | I Will Not Allow Others Who Look Like Me To Tell Me:

What I Love About My Skin Today: | I Will Not Allow Others Who Do Not Look Like Me To Tell Me:

I Am Proud To Be: | It Is Okay If I Am The Only One:

I Am Beautiful/Good Looking Because: | It Is Okay If I Do Not Fit Into:

The Last Negative Comment I Received Towards My Appearance/Personality And My Thoughts Towards The Comment: | Everyday I Am Learning To Accept:

How Did I Respond Towards The Comment Made In The Previous Prompt? | Just Because I Don't/Do

_____, Doesn't Mean I:

It Is Okay For Me To Like _____
And Still Be:

113

It Does Not Matter Who Treats Me Differently When I Know God Sees Me And Loves Me The Way He Created Me.

It Hurts Me To Hear....

Loving Me For Who I Am

Date: Mood:

What I Love About My Hair Today: I Will Not Allow Others Who Look Like
                                               Me To Tell Me:

What I Love About My Skin Today: I Will Not Allow Others Who Do Not
                                               Look Like Me To Tell Me:

I Am Proud To Be: It Is Okay If I Am The Only One:

I Am Beautiful/Good Looking   It Is Okay If I Do Not Fit Into:
Because:

The Last Negative Comment I   Everyday I Am Learning To Accept:
Received Towards My Appearance/
Personality And My Thoughts
Towards The Comment:

How Did I Respond Towards The   Just Because I Don't/Do
Comment Made In The Previous
Prompt?   _____, Doesn't Mean I:

It Is Okay For Me To Like
_____
And Still Be:

When Others Look At Me, They See A Person Who Is Competent, Confident, And Beautiful.

116

Loving Me For Who I Am

Date: Mood:

What I Love About My Hair Today: | I Will Not Allow Others Who Look Like Me To Tell Me:

What I Love About My Skin Today: | I Will Not Allow Others Who Do Not Look Like Me To Tell Me:

I Am Proud To Be: | It Is Okay If I Am The Only One:

I Am Beautiful/Good Looking Because: | It Is Okay If I Do Not Fit Into:

The Last Negative Comment I Received Towards My Appearance/Personality And My Thoughts Towards The Comment: | Everyday I Am Learning To Accept:

How Did I Respond Towards The Comment Made In The Previous Prompt? | Just Because I Don't/Do

_____, Doesn't Mean I:

It Is Okay For Me To Like

_____

And Still Be:

Loving Me For Who I Am

Date: Mood:

What I Love About My Hair Today: I Will Not Allow Others Who Look Like Me To Tell Me:

What I Love About My Skin Today: I Will Not Allow Others Who Do Not Look Like Me To Tell Me:

I Am Proud To Be: It Is Okay If I Am The Only One:

I Am Beautiful/Good Looking Because: It Is Okay If I Do Not Fit Into:

The Last Negative Comment I Received Towards My Appearance/Personality And My Thoughts Towards The Comment: Everyday I Am Learning To Accept:

How Did I Respond Towards The Comment Made In The Previous Prompt?   Just Because I Don't/Do

_____, Doesn't Mean I:

It Is Okay For Me To Like
_____
And Still Be:

I Will Not Force Anyone To Love A Diamond.

I Am The Representation That I Look For.

Loving Me For Who I Am

Date: Mood:

What I Love About My Hair Today: I Will Not Allow Others Who Look Like Me To Tell Me:

What I Love About My Skin Today: I Will Not Allow Others Who Do Not Look Like Me To Tell Me:

I Am Proud To Be: It Is Okay If I Am The Only One:

I Am Beautiful/Good Looking Because: It Is Okay If I Do Not Fit Into:

The Last Negative Comment I Received Towards My Appearance/Personality And My Thoughts Towards The Comment: Everyday I Am Learning To Accept:

How Did I Respond Towards The Comment Made In The Previous Prompt?   Just Because I Don't/Do

_____, Doesn't Mean I:

It Is Okay For Me To Like

_____

And Still Be:

There Is A Reason Why I Am Going Through This. I Am To Come Out Of This Stronger.

My Thoughts

Loving Me For Who I Am

Date: Mood:

What I Love About My Hair Today: I Will Not Allow Others Who Look Like Me To Tell Me:

What I Love About My Skin Today: I Will Not Allow Others Who Do Not Look Like Me To Tell Me:

I Am Proud To Be: It Is Okay If I Am The Only One:

I Am Beautiful/Good Looking Because: It Is Okay If I Do Not Fit Into:

The Last Negative Comment I Received Towards My Appearance/Personality And My Thoughts Towards The Comment: Everyday I Am Learning To Accept:

How Did I Respond Towards The Comment Made In The Previous Prompt?   Just Because I Don't/Do

_____, Doesn't Mean I:

It Is Okay For Me To Like

_____

And Still Be:

I Consider People Of All Races And Religions To Be My Friends.

Loving Me For Who I Am

Date: Mood:

I Am Beautiful. I Am Whole. I Am Enough. I Am Loved. I Am Needed.

What I Love About My Hair Today:	I Will Not Allow Others Who Look Like Me To Tell Me:
What I Love About My Skin Today:	I Will Not Allow Others Who Do Not Look Like Me To Tell Me:
I Am Proud To Be:	It Is Okay If I Am The Only One:
I Am Beautiful/Good Looking Because:	It Is Okay If I Do Not Fit Into:
The Last Negative Comment I Received Towards My Appearance/Personality And My Thoughts Towards The Comment:	Everyday I Am Learning To Accept:
How Did I Respond Towards The Comment Made In The Previous Prompt?	Just Because I Don't/Do _____, Doesn't Mean I:
It Is Okay For Me To Like _____ And Still Be:	

124

In My Skin I Win.

It Does Not Matter What They Love, What Matters Is What I Love.

Loving Me For Who I Am

Date: Mood:

What I Love About My Hair Today: I Will Not Allow Others Who Look Like Me To Tell Me:

What I Love About My Skin Today: I Will Not Allow Others Who Do Not Look Like Me To Tell Me:

I Am Proud To Be: It Is Okay If I Am The Only One:

I Am Beautiful/Good Looking Because: It Is Okay If I Do Not Fit Into:

The Last Negative Comment I Received Towards My Appearance/Personality And My Thoughts Towards The Comment: Everyday I Am Learning To Accept:

How Did I Respond Towards The Comment Made In The Previous Prompt?   Just Because I Don't/Do

_____, Doesn't Mean I:

It Is Okay For Me To Like

_____

And Still Be:

Loving Me For Who I Am

Date: Mood:

What I Love About My Hair Today: I Will Not Allow Others Who Look Like Me To Tell Me:

What I Love About My Skin Today: I Will Not Allow Others Who Do Not Look Like Me To Tell Me:

I Am Proud To Be: It Is Okay If I Am The Only One:

I Am Beautiful/Good Looking Because: It Is Okay If I Do Not Fit Into:

The Last Negative Comment I Received Towards My Appearance/Personality And My Thoughts Towards The Comment: Everyday I Am Learning To Accept:

How Did I Respond Towards The Comment Made In The Previous Prompt?   Just Because I Don't/Do

_____, Doesn't Mean I:

It Is Okay For Me To Like _____

And Still Be:

I Refuse To Let Insults, Derogatory Comments, And Racial Slurs Drag Me Down.

128

Loving Me For Who I Am

Date: Mood:

What I Love About My Hair Today: I Will Not Allow Others Who Look Like Me To Tell Me:

What I Love About My Skin Today: I Will Not Allow Others Who Do Not Look Like Me To Tell Me:

I Am Proud To Be: It Is Okay If I Am The Only One:

I Am Beautiful/Good Looking Because: It Is Okay If I Do Not Fit Into:

The Last Negative Comment I Received Towards My Appearance/Personality And My Thoughts Towards The Comment: Everyday I Am Learning To Accept:

How Did I Respond Towards The Comment Made In The Previous Prompt?   Just Because I Don't/Do _____, Doesn't Mean I:

It Is Okay For Me To Like _____ And Still Be:

I Am Beautiful In All Ways, In And Out, From The Color Of My Skin To The Genuine Kindness Of My Heart.

I Am More Than Good Enough.

I Am Going To Use My Voice To....

Loving Me For Who I Am

Date: Mood:

What I Love About My Hair Today: I Will Not Allow Others Who Look Like Me To Tell Me:

What I Love About My Skin Today: I Will Not Allow Others Who Do Not Look Like Me To Tell Me:

I Am Proud To Be: It Is Okay If I Am The Only One:

I Am Beautiful/Good Looking Because: It Is Okay If I Do Not Fit Into:

The Last Negative Comment I Received Towards My Appearance/Personality And My Thoughts Towards The Comment: Everyday I Am Learning To Accept:

How Did I Respond Towards The Comment Made In The Previous Prompt?   Just Because I Don't/Do

_____, Doesn't Mean I:

It Is Okay For Me To Like

_____

And Still Be:

132

Loving Me For Who I Am

Date: Mood:

What I Love About My Hair Today: I Will Not Allow Others Who Look Like Me To Tell Me:

What I Love About My Skin Today: I Will Not Allow Others Who Do Not Look Like Me To Tell Me:

I Am Proud To Be: It Is Okay If I Am The Only One:

I Am Beautiful/Good Looking Because: It Is Okay If I Do Not Fit Into:

The Last Negative Comment I Received Towards My Appearance/Personality And My Thoughts Towards The Comment: Everyday I Am Learning To Accept:

How Did I Respond Towards The Comment Made In The Previous Prompt?   Just Because I Don't/Do

_____, Doesn't Mean I:

It Is Okay For Me To Like

_____

And Still Be:

I Am Grateful For Being Born Into My Heritage That's Rich With History And Culture.

133

Loving Me For Who I Am

Date: Mood:

What I Love About My Hair Today: I Will Not Allow Others Who Look Like Me To Tell Me:

What I Love About My Skin Today: I Will Not Allow Others Who Do Not Look Like Me To Tell Me:

I Am Proud To Be: It Is Okay If I Am The Only One:

I Am Beautiful/Good Looking Because: It Is Okay If I Do Not Fit Into:

The Last Negative Comment I Received Towards My Appearance/Personality And My Thoughts Towards The Comment: Everyday I Am Learning To Accept:

How Did I Respond Towards The Comment Made In The Previous Prompt?   Just Because I Don't/Do

_____, Doesn't Mean I:

It Is Okay For Me To Like

_____

And Still Be:

I Mindfully Celebrate The Culture Of My Ancestors And My Family's Country Of Origin.

The Way
I Talk To
Myself Is
With Love And
Admiration.

No One Can Convince Me That I Am Not Amazing.

Loving Me For Who I Am

Date: Mood:

What I Love About My Hair Today: I Will Not Allow Others Who Look Like Me To Tell Me:

What I Love About My Skin Today: I Will Not Allow Others Who Do Not Look Like Me To Tell Me:

I Am Proud To Be: It Is Okay If I Am The Only One:

I Am Beautiful/Good Looking Because: It Is Okay If I Do Not Fit Into:

The Last Negative Comment I Received Towards My Appearance/Personality And My Thoughts Towards The Comment: Everyday I Am Learning To Accept:

How Did I Respond Towards The Comment Made In The Previous Prompt?   Just Because I Don't/Do _____, Doesn't Mean I:

It Is Okay For Me To Like
_____
And Still Be:

I Am Becoming A Better Version Of Myself One Day At A Time.

Loving Me For Who I Am

Date: Mood:

What I Love About My Hair Today: I Will Not Allow Others Who Look Like
                                                         Me To Tell Me:

What I Love About My Skin Today: I Will Not Allow Others Who Do Not
                                                         Look Like Me To Tell Me:

I Am Proud To Be: It Is Okay If I Am The Only One:

I Am Beautiful/Good Looking   It Is Okay If I Do Not Fit Into:
Because:

The Last Negative Comment I   Everyday I Am Learning To Accept:
Received Towards My Appearance/
Personality And My Thoughts
Towards The Comment:

How Did I Respond Towards The   Just Because I Don't/Do
Comment Made In The Previous
Prompt?   _____, Doesn't Mean I:

It Is Okay For Me To Like

_____
And Still Be:

I Will Always Show Unconditional Love Towards Myself.

Loving Me For Who I Am

Date: Mood:

What I Love About My Hair Today: I Will Not Allow Others Who Look Like Me To Tell Me:

What I Love About My Skin Today: I Will Not Allow Others Who Do Not Look Like Me To Tell Me:

I Am Proud To Be: It Is Okay If I Am The Only One:

I Am Beautiful/Good Looking Because: It Is Okay If I Do Not Fit Into:

The Last Negative Comment I Received Towards My Appearance/Personality And My Thoughts Towards The Comment: Everyday I Am Learning To Accept:

How Did I Respond Towards The Comment Made In The Previous Prompt?   Just Because I Don't/Do

_____, Doesn't Mean I:

It Is Okay For Me To Like

_____

And Still Be:

I Will Always Walk On The Path That Promotes Inner Healing.

How Do I Show Love To Myself And Those Who Look Like Me?

They See Me. They See Me Because I Am Flourishing As Me.

Loving Me For Who I Am

Date: Mood:

What I Love About My Hair Today: I Will Not Allow Others Who Look Like Me To Tell Me:

What I Love About My Skin Today: I Will Not Allow Others Who Do Not Look Like Me To Tell Me:

I Am Proud To Be: It Is Okay If I Am The Only One:

I Am Beautiful/Good Looking Because: It Is Okay If I Do Not Fit Into:

The Last Negative Comment I Received Towards My Appearance/Personality And My Thoughts Towards The Comment: Everyday I Am Learning To Accept:

How Did I Respond Towards The Comment Made In The Previous Prompt?   Just Because I Don't/Do _____, Doesn't Mean I:

It Is Okay For Me To Like
_____
And Still Be:

I Eliminate All Negative Thoughts About Myself.

Loving Me For Who I Am

Date: Mood:

What I Love About My Hair Today: I Will Not Allow Others Who Look Like Me To Tell Me:

What I Love About My Skin Today: I Will Not Allow Others Who Do Not Look Like Me To Tell Me:

I Am Proud To Be: It Is Okay If I Am The Only One:

I Am Beautiful/Good Looking Because: It Is Okay If I Do Not Fit Into:

The Last Negative Comment I Received Towards My Appearance/Personality And My Thoughts Towards The Comment: Everyday I Am Learning To Accept:

How Did I Respond Towards The Comment Made In The Previous Prompt?   Just Because I Don't/Do

_____, Doesn't Mean I:

It Is Okay For Me To Like

_____

And Still Be:

> I Know That Loving Myself Means Loving Others Who Also Look Just Like Me.

Loving Me For Who I Am

Date: Mood:

What I Love About My Hair Today: I Will Not Allow Others Who Look Like Me To Tell Me:

What I Love About My Skin Today: I Will Not Allow Others Who Do Not Look Like Me To Tell Me:

I Am Proud To Be: It Is Okay If I Am The Only One:

I Am Beautiful/Good Looking Because: It Is Okay If I Do Not Fit Into:

The Last Negative Comment I Received Towards My Appearance/Personality And My Thoughts Towards The Comment: Everyday I Am Learning To Accept:

How Did I Respond Towards The Comment Made In The Previous Prompt?   Just Because I Don't/Do _____, Doesn't Mean I:

It Is Okay For Me To Like
_____
And Still Be:

I Stand Up To Acts Of Colorism To Let People Know That It Is Wrong.

My Thoughts

Loving Me For Who I Am

Date: Mood:

What I Love About My Hair Today: I Will Not Allow Others Who Look Like Me To Tell Me:

What I Love About My Skin Today: I Will Not Allow Others Who Do Not Look Like Me To Tell Me:

I Am Proud To Be: It Is Okay If I Am The Only One:

I Am Beautiful/Good Looking Because: It Is Okay If I Do Not Fit Into:

The Last Negative Comment I Received Towards My Appearance/Personality And My Thoughts Towards The Comment: Everyday I Am Learning To Accept:

How Did I Respond Towards The Comment Made In The Previous Prompt?   Just Because I Don't/Do

_____, Doesn't Mean I:

It Is Okay For Me To Like

_____

And Still Be:

I Am The Standard Of Beauty. I Set The Standard Of Beauty.

146

Loving Me For Who I Am

Date: Mood:

What I Love About My Hair Today: I Will Not Allow Others Who Look Like Me To Tell Me:

What I Love About My Skin Today: I Will Not Allow Others Who Do Not Look Like Me To Tell Me:

I Am Proud To Be: It Is Okay If I Am The Only One:

I Am Beautiful/Good Looking Because: It Is Okay If I Do Not Fit Into:

The Last Negative Comment I Received Towards My Appearance/Personality And My Thoughts Towards The Comment: Everyday I Am Learning To Accept:

How Did I Respond Towards The Comment Made In The Previous Prompt?   Just Because I Don't/Do

_____, Doesn't Mean I:

It Is Okay For Me To Like

_____

And Still Be:

I Am At Peace With Myself. I Am Comfortable In My Own Skin.

No One Can Take Me Away From My Heritage.

There Is Nothing Wrong With The Way I Speak.

Loving Me For Who I Am

Date: Mood:

What I Love About My Hair Today: I Will Not Allow Others Who Look Like Me To Tell Me:

What I Love About My Skin Today: I Will Not Allow Others Who Do Not Look Like Me To Tell Me:

I Am Proud To Be: It Is Okay If I Am The Only One:

I Am Beautiful/Good Looking Because: It Is Okay If I Do Not Fit Into:

The Last Negative Comment I Received Towards My Appearance/Personality And My Thoughts Towards The Comment: Everyday I Am Learning To Accept:

How Did I Respond Towards The Comment Made In The Previous Prompt?   Just Because I Don't/Do _____, Doesn't Mean I:

It Is Okay For Me To Like _____ And Still Be:

Who Can I Talk To About Colorism?

Loving Me For Who I Am

Date: Mood:

What I Love About My Hair Today: I Will Not Allow Others Who Look Like Me To Tell Me:

What I Love About My Skin Today: I Will Not Allow Others Who Do Not Look Like Me To Tell Me:

I Am Proud To Be: It Is Okay If I Am The Only One:

I Am Beautiful/Good Looking Because: It Is Okay If I Do Not Fit Into:

The Last Negative Comment I Received Towards My Appearance/Personality And My Thoughts Towards The Comment: Everyday I Am Learning To Accept:

How Did I Respond Towards The Comment Made In The Previous Prompt?   Just Because I Don't/Do

_____, Doesn't Mean I:

It Is Okay For Me To Like

_____

And Still Be:

Loving Me For Who I Am

Date: Mood:

What I Love About My Hair Today: I Will Not Allow Others Who Look Like Me To Tell Me:

What I Love About My Skin Today: I Will Not Allow Others Who Do Not Look Like Me To Tell Me:

I Am Proud To Be: It Is Okay If I Am The Only One:

I Am Beautiful/Good Looking Because: It Is Okay If I Do Not Fit Into:

The Last Negative Comment I Received Towards My Appearance/Personality And My Thoughts Towards The Comment: Everyday I Am Learning To Accept:

How Did I Respond Towards The Comment Made In The Previous Prompt?   Just Because I Don't/Do

_____, Doesn't Mean I:

It Is Okay For Me To Like

_____

And Still Be:

I Encourage Everyone Who Looks Like Me To Thrive.

Even When They Make Fun Of Me, I Will Always Show Them Love.

My Thoughts

Loving Me For Who I Am

Date: Mood:

What I Love About My Hair Today: I Will Not Allow Others Who Look Like Me To Tell Me:

What I Love About My Skin Today: I Will Not Allow Others Who Do Not Look Like Me To Tell Me:

I Am Proud To Be: It Is Okay If I Am The Only One:

I Am Beautiful/Good Looking Because: It Is Okay If I Do Not Fit Into:

The Last Negative Comment I Received Towards My Appearance/Personality And My Thoughts Towards The Comment: Everyday I Am Learning To Accept:

How Did I Respond Towards The Comment Made In The Previous Prompt?   Just Because I Don't/Do

_____, Doesn't Mean I:

It Is Okay For Me To Like
_____
And Still Be:

I Am Comfortable And Confident In My Own Skin.

Loving Me For Who I Am

Date: Mood:

What I Love About My Hair Today: I Will Not Allow Others Who Look Like Me To Tell Me:

What I Love About My Skin Today: I Will Not Allow Others Who Do Not Look Like Me To Tell Me:

I Am Proud To Be: It Is Okay If I Am The Only One:

I Am Beautiful/Good Looking Because: It Is Okay If I Do Not Fit Into:

The Last Negative Comment I Received Towards My Appearance/Personality And My Thoughts Towards The Comment: Everyday I Am Learning To Accept:

How Did I Respond Towards The Comment Made In The Previous Prompt?   Just Because I Don't/Do

_____, Doesn't Mean I:

It Is Okay For Me To Like

_____

And Still Be:

I Am The Only One Who Can Fully Stand Up And Show Up For Me.

Loving Me For Who I Am

Date: Mood:

What I Love About My Hair Today: I Will Not Allow Others Who Look Like Me To Tell Me:

What I Love About My Skin Today: I Will Not Allow Others Who Do Not Look Like Me To Tell Me:

I Am Proud To Be: It Is Okay If I Am The Only One:

I Am Beautiful/Good Looking Because: It Is Okay If I Do Not Fit Into:

The Last Negative Comment I Received Towards My Appearance/Personality And My Thoughts Towards The Comment: Everyday I Am Learning To Accept:

How Did I Respond Towards The Comment Made In The Previous Prompt?   Just Because I Don't/Do _____, Doesn't Mean I:

It Is Okay For Me To Like
_____
And Still Be:

Every Day, I Vow To Take Pride In My Heritage And My Cultural Roots.

158

There Is Just Something Special About Me That They Will Never Get To Experience.

I No Longer Tolerate Hateful Messages Towards My Skin, Body And/Or Language. I Stand Up For People Who Look Just Like Me.

Loving Me For Who I Am

Date: Mood:

What I Love About My Hair Today:

I Will Not Allow Others Who Look Like Me To Tell Me:

What I Love About My Skin Today:

I Will Not Allow Others Who Do Not Look Like Me To Tell Me:

I Am Proud To Be:

It Is Okay If I Am The Only One:

I Am Beautiful/Good Looking Because:

It Is Okay If I Do Not Fit Into:

The Last Negative Comment I Received Towards My Appearance/Personality And My Thoughts Towards The Comment:

Everyday I Am Learning To Accept:

How Did I Respond Towards The Comment Made In The Previous Prompt?

Just Because I Don't/Do

_____, Doesn't Mean I:

It Is Okay For Me To Like

_____

And Still Be:

I Truly Love All Of Me.

Loving Me For Who I Am

Date: Mood:

What I Love About My Hair Today: I Will Not Allow Others Who Look Like Me To Tell Me:

What I Love About My Skin Today: I Will Not Allow Others Who Do Not Look Like Me To Tell Me:

I Am Proud To Be: It Is Okay If I Am The Only One:

I Am Beautiful/Good Looking Because: It Is Okay If I Do Not Fit Into:

The Last Negative Comment I Received Towards My Appearance/Personality And My Thoughts Towards The Comment: Everyday I Am Learning To Accept:

How Did I Respond Towards The Comment Made In The Previous Prompt?   Just Because I Don't/Do

_____, Doesn't Mean I:

It Is Okay For Me To Like

_____

And Still Be:

It Does Not Matter How I Look Because I Manage To Always Exude Beauty.

Loving Me For Who I Am

Date: Mood:

What I Love About My Hair Today: I Will Not Allow Others Who Look Like Me To Tell Me:

What I Love About My Skin Today: I Will Not Allow Others Who Do Not Look Like Me To Tell Me:

I Am Proud To Be: It Is Okay If I Am The Only One:

I Am Beautiful/Good Looking Because: It Is Okay If I Do Not Fit Into:

The Last Negative Comment I Received Towards My Appearance/Personality And My Thoughts Towards The Comment: Everyday I Am Learning To Accept:

How Did I Respond Towards The Comment Made In The Previous Prompt?   Just Because I Don't/Do

_____, Doesn't Mean I:

It Is Okay For Me To Like

_____

And Still Be:

I Have Stopped Hating My Skin Tone And Have Learned To Love The Way I Look.

A List Of People In My Family Who Treat Me Differently Because Of How I Look....

They Tried To Keep Me From The Best, Meanwhile The Best Found Me.

Loving Me For Who I Am

Date: Mood:

What I Love About My Hair Today: I Will Not Allow Others Who Look Like Me To Tell Me:

What I Love About My Skin Today: I Will Not Allow Others Who Do Not Look Like Me To Tell Me:

I Am Proud To Be: It Is Okay If I Am The Only One:

I Am Beautiful/Good Looking Because: It Is Okay If I Do Not Fit Into:

The Last Negative Comment I Received Towards My Appearance/Personality And My Thoughts Towards The Comment: Everyday I Am Learning To Accept:

How Did I Respond Towards The Comment Made In The Previous Prompt?   Just Because I Don't/Do _____, Doesn't Mean I:

It Is Okay For Me To Like _____
And Still Be:

Loving Me For Who I Am

Date: Mood:

What I Love About My Hair Today: I Will Not Allow Others Who Look Like Me To Tell Me:

What I Love About My Skin Today: I Will Not Allow Others Who Do Not Look Like Me To Tell Me:

I Am Proud To Be: It Is Okay If I Am The Only One:

I Am Beautiful/Good Looking Because: It Is Okay If I Do Not Fit Into:

The Last Negative Comment I Received Towards My Appearance/Personality And My Thoughts Towards The Comment: Everyday I Am Learning To Accept:

How Did I Respond Towards The Comment Made In The Previous Prompt?   Just Because I Don't/Do

_____, Doesn't Mean I:

It Is Okay For Me To Like

_____

And Still Be:

Loving Me For Who I Am

Date: Mood:

What I Love About My Hair Today: I Will Not Allow Others Who Look Like Me To Tell Me:

What I Love About My Skin Today: I Will Not Allow Others Who Do Not Look Like Me To Tell Me:

I Am Proud To Be: It Is Okay If I Am The Only One:

I Am Beautiful/Good Looking Because: It Is Okay If I Do Not Fit Into:

The Last Negative Comment I Received Towards My Appearance/Personality And My Thoughts Towards The Comment: Everyday I Am Learning To Accept:

How Did I Respond Towards The Comment Made In The Previous Prompt?   Just Because I Don't/Do _____, Doesn't Mean I:

It Is Okay For Me To Like _____ And Still Be:

When I Look At Myself I Only See Beauty.

It Took Me A Minute But I Have Grown To Love The Parts Of Me They Tried To Get Me To Change.

I Will Not Treat Anyone Differently Because Of The Color Of Their Skin.

Loving Me For Who I Am

Date: Mood:

What I Love About My Hair Today: I Will Not Allow Others Who Look Like Me To Tell Me:

What I Love About My Skin Today: I Will Not Allow Others Who Do Not Look Like Me To Tell Me:

I Am Proud To Be: It Is Okay If I Am The Only One:

I Am Beautiful/Good Looking Because: It Is Okay If I Do Not Fit Into:

The Last Negative Comment I Received Towards My Appearance/Personality And My Thoughts Towards The Comment: Everyday I Am Learning To Accept:

How Did I Respond Towards The Comment Made In The Previous Prompt?   Just Because I Don't/Do

_____, Doesn't Mean I:

It Is Okay For Me To Like

_____

And Still Be:

I Know That I Have Every Right To Be Happy And To Pursue My Dreams.

Loving Me For Who I Am

Date: Mood:

What I Love About My Hair Today: I Will Not Allow Others Who Look Like Me To Tell Me:

What I Love About My Skin Today: I Will Not Allow Others Who Do Not Look Like Me To Tell Me:

I Am Proud To Be: It Is Okay If I Am The Only One:

I Am Beautiful/Good Looking Because: It Is Okay If I Do Not Fit Into:

The Last Negative Comment I Received Towards My Appearance/Personality And My Thoughts Towards The Comment: Everyday I Am Learning To Accept:

How Did I Respond Towards The Comment Made In The Previous Prompt?   Just Because I Don't/Do

_____, Doesn't Mean I:

It Is Okay For Me To Like

_____

And Still Be:

I Am Happy And Content With Myself.

Loving Me For Who I Am

Date: Mood:

What I Love About My Hair Today: | I Will Not Allow Others Who Look Like Me To Tell Me:

What I Love About My Skin Today: | I Will Not Allow Others Who Do Not Look Like Me To Tell Me:

I Am Proud To Be: | It Is Okay If I Am The Only One:

I Am Beautiful/Good Looking Because: | It Is Okay If I Do Not Fit Into:

The Last Negative Comment I Received Towards My Appearance/Personality And My Thoughts Towards The Comment: | Everyday I Am Learning To Accept:

How Did I Respond Towards The Comment Made In The Previous Prompt? | Just Because I Don't/Do _____, Doesn't Mean I:

It Is Okay For Me To Like _____ And Still Be:

I Do Not Need Anyone's Validation.

Why Do I Wish I Looked Different?

What Is Wrong With The Way I Look?

I Want To Belong. I Want To Be Accepted, But Only For Who I Am And Not For What Anyone Wants Me To Conform To.

Loving Me For Who I Am

Date: Mood:

What I Love About My Hair Today: I Will Not Allow Others Who Look Like
                                                   Me To Tell Me:

What I Love About My Skin Today: I Will Not Allow Others Who Do Not
                                                   Look Like Me To Tell Me:

I Am Proud To Be: It Is Okay If I Am The Only One:

I Am Beautiful/Good Looking   It Is Okay If I Do Not Fit Into:
Because:

The Last Negative Comment I   Everyday I Am Learning To Accept:
Received Towards My Appearance/
Personality And My Thoughts
Towards The Comment:

How Did I Respond Towards The   Just Because I Don't/Do
Comment Made In The Previous
Prompt?   _____, Doesn't Mean I:

It Is Okay For Me To Like

_____

And Still Be:

Loving Me For Who I Am

Date: Mood:

What I Love About My Hair Today: I Will Not Allow Others Who Look Like Me To Tell Me:

What I Love About My Skin Today: I Will Not Allow Others Who Do Not Look Like Me To Tell Me:

I Am Proud To Be: It Is Okay If I Am The Only One:

I Am Beautiful/Good Looking Because: It Is Okay If I Do Not Fit Into:

The Last Negative Comment I Received Towards My Appearance/Personality And My Thoughts Towards The Comment: Everyday I Am Learning To Accept:

How Did I Respond Towards The Comment Made In The Previous Prompt?   Just Because I Don't/Do _____, Doesn't Mean I:

It Is Okay For Me To Like _____ And Still Be:

I Radiate In My Own Skin. I Can Never Shine Being Someone I Am Not.

Loving Me For Who I Am

Date: Mood:

What I Love About My Hair Today: I Will Not Allow Others Who Look Like Me To Tell Me:

What I Love About My Skin Today: I Will Not Allow Others Who Do Not Look Like Me To Tell Me:

I Am Proud To Be: It Is Okay If I Am The Only One:

I Am Beautiful/Good Looking Because: It Is Okay If I Do Not Fit Into:

The Last Negative Comment I Received Towards My Appearance/Personality And My Thoughts Towards The Comment: Everyday I Am Learning To Accept:

How Did I Respond Towards The Comment Made In The Previous Prompt?   Just Because I Don't/Do _____, Doesn't Mean I:

It Is Okay For Me To Like _____ And Still Be:

The More I Let Go Of My Insecurities And Self-Doubt, The Better I Feel.

178

I Will Not Be Made To Feel Like An Outcast By Those Who Claim To Be Friends/Family.

Some Say I Am Not Enough Of This Or I Am Too Much Of That But God Gave Me More Than Enough To Thrive And Be Accepted By Those Who Will Love Me For Me.

Loving Me For Who I Am

Date: Mood:

What I Love About My Hair Today: I Will Not Allow Others Who Look Like Me To Tell Me:

What I Love About My Skin Today: I Will Not Allow Others Who Do Not Look Like Me To Tell Me:

I Am Proud To Be: It Is Okay If I Am The Only One:

I Am Beautiful/Good Looking Because: It Is Okay If I Do Not Fit Into:

The Last Negative Comment I Received Towards My Appearance/Personality And My Thoughts Towards The Comment: Everyday I Am Learning To Accept:

How Did I Respond Towards The Comment Made In The Previous Prompt?   Just Because I Don't/Do

_____, Doesn't Mean I:

It Is Okay For Me To Like

_____

And Still Be:

I Am Braver And Stronger Than I Think. My Potential Is Limitless.

Loving Me For Who I Am

Date: Mood:

What I Love About My Hair Today: | I Will Not Allow Others Who Look Like Me To Tell Me:

What I Love About My Skin Today: | I Will Not Allow Others Who Do Not Look Like Me To Tell Me:

I Am Proud To Be: | It Is Okay If I Am The Only One:

I Am Beautiful/Good Looking Because: | It Is Okay If I Do Not Fit Into:

The Last Negative Comment I Received Towards My Appearance/Personality And My Thoughts Towards The Comment: | Everyday I Am Learning To Accept:

How Did I Respond Towards The Comment Made In The Previous Prompt? | Just Because I Don't/Do _____, Doesn't Mean I:

It Is Okay For Me To Like _____ And Still Be:

People's Respect.

Loving Me For Who I Am

Date: Mood:

What I Love About My Hair Today: I Will Not Allow Others Who Look Like Me To Tell Me:

What I Love About My Skin Today: I Will Not Allow Others Who Do Not Look Like Me To Tell Me:

I Am Proud To Be: It Is Okay If I Am The Only One:

I Am Beautiful/Good Looking Because: It Is Okay If I Do Not Fit Into:

The Last Negative Comment I Received Towards My Appearance/Personality And My Thoughts Towards The Comment: Everyday I Am Learning To Accept:

How Did I Respond Towards The Comment Made In The Previous Prompt?   Just Because I Don't/Do

_____, Doesn't Mean I:

It Is Okay For Me To Like

_____

And Still Be:

I Am The Only Person Who Can Tell Me What I Am.

My Thoughts

How Do I Gain A Better Self Image?

Loving Me For Who I Am

Date: Mood:

What I Love About My Hair Today: I Will Not Allow Others Who Look Like Me To Tell Me:

What I Love About My Skin Today: I Will Not Allow Others Who Do Not Look Like Me To Tell Me:

I Am Proud To Be: It Is Okay If I Am The Only One:

I Am Beautiful/Good Looking Because: It Is Okay If I Do Not Fit Into:

The Last Negative Comment I Received Towards My Appearance/Personality And My Thoughts Towards The Comment: Everyday I Am Learning To Accept:

How Did I Respond Towards The Comment Made In The Previous Prompt?   Just Because I Don't/Do _____, Doesn't Mean I:

It Is Okay For Me To Like _____ And Still Be:

My Skin Tone Is Not An Issue For Me And Those Who Love Me.

Loving Me For Who I Am

Date: Mood:

What I Love About My Hair Today: | I Will Not Allow Others Who Look Like Me To Tell Me:

What I Love About My Skin Today: | I Will Not Allow Others Who Do Not Look Like Me To Tell Me:

I Am Proud To Be: | It Is Okay If I Am The Only One:

I Am Beautiful/Good Looking Because: | It Is Okay If I Do Not Fit Into:

The Last Negative Comment I Received Towards My Appearance/Personality And My Thoughts Towards The Comment: | Everyday I Am Learning To Accept:

How Did I Respond Towards The Comment Made In The Previous Prompt? | Just Because I Don't/Do

_____, Doesn't Mean I:

It Is Okay For Me To Like

_____

And Still Be:

Loving Me For Who I Am

Date: Mood:

What I Love About My Hair Today: I Will Not Allow Others Who Look Like Me To Tell Me:

What I Love About My Skin Today: I Will Not Allow Others Who Do Not Look Like Me To Tell Me:

I Am Proud To Be: It Is Okay If I Am The Only One:

I Am Beautiful/Good Looking Because: It Is Okay If I Do Not Fit Into:

The Last Negative Comment I Received Towards My Appearance/Personality And My Thoughts Towards The Comment: Everyday I Am Learning To Accept:

How Did I Respond Towards The Comment Made In The Previous Prompt?   Just Because I Don't/Do

_____, Doesn't Mean I:

It Is Okay For Me To Like _____

And Still Be:

The Standard Of Beauty That They Try To Measure Me Against Has Nothing To Do With Who I Am Or Where I Come From.

I Am Waiting On Me To Accept Myself.

Loving Me For Who I Am

Date: Mood:

What I Love About My Hair Today:

I Will Not Allow Others Who Look Like Me To Tell Me:

What I Love About My Skin Today:

I Will Not Allow Others Who Do Not Look Like Me To Tell Me:

I Am Proud To Be:

It Is Okay If I Am The Only One:

I Am Beautiful/Good Looking Because:

It Is Okay If I Do Not Fit Into:

The Last Negative Comment I Received Towards My Appearance/Personality And My Thoughts Towards The Comment:

Everyday I Am Learning To Accept:

How Did I Respond Towards The Comment Made In The Previous Prompt?

Just Because I Don't/Do

_____, Doesn't Mean I:

It Is Okay For Me To Like
_____
And Still Be:

I Decided That I Will Define What Is Beautiful For Me.

Loving Me For Who I Am

Date: Mood:

What I Love About My Hair Today: I Will Not Allow Others Who Look Like
                                                   Me To Tell Me:

What I Love About My Skin Today: I Will Not Allow Others Who Do Not
                                                   Look Like Me To Tell Me:

I Am Proud To Be: It Is Okay If I Am The Only One:

I Am Beautiful/Good Looking   It Is Okay If I Do Not Fit Into:
Because:

The Last Negative Comment I   Everyday I Am Learning To Accept:
Received Towards My Appearance/
Personality And My Thoughts
Towards The Comment:

How Did I Respond Towards The   Just Because I Don't/Do
Comment Made In The Previous
Prompt?   _____ _____, Doesn't Mean I:

It Is Okay For Me To Like
_____
And Still Be:

I Will No Longer Struggle To Accept Who I Am.

Loving Me For Who I Am

Date: Mood:

What I Love About My Hair Today: I Will Not Allow Others Who Look Like Me To Tell Me:

What I Love About My Skin Today: I Will Not Allow Others Who Do Not Look Like Me To Tell Me:

I Am Proud To Be: It Is Okay If I Am The Only One:

I Am Beautiful/Good Looking Because: It Is Okay If I Do Not Fit Into:

The Last Negative Comment I Received Towards My Appearance/Personality And My Thoughts Towards The Comment: Everyday I Am Learning To Accept:

How Did I Respond Towards The Comment Made In The Previous Prompt?   Just Because I Don't/Do

_____, Doesn't Mean I:

It Is Okay For Me To Like _____
And Still Be:

The Opinions I Have Of Myself Are The Ones That Matter The Most.

My Thoughts

I Want To Feel Protected And Wanted In My Own Skin.

Loving Me For Who I Am

Date:	Mood:

What I Love About My Hair Today:	I Will Not Allow Others Who Look Like Me To Tell Me:

What I Love About My Skin Today:	I Will Not Allow Others Who Do Not Look Like Me To Tell Me:

I Am Proud To Be:	It Is Okay If I Am The Only One:

I Am Beautiful/Good Looking Because:	It Is Okay If I Do Not Fit Into:

The Last Negative Comment I Received Towards My Appearance/ Personality And My Thoughts Towards The Comment:	Everyday I Am Learning To Accept:

How Did I Respond Towards The Comment Made In The Previous Prompt?	Just Because I Don't/Do

_____, Doesn't Mean I:

It Is Okay For Me To Like

_____
And Still Be:

Not Only Do I Stand Up For Myself But The People Who Love Me Will Stand Up For Me As Well.

Loving Me For Who I Am

Date: Mood:

What I Love About My Hair Today: I Will Not Allow Others Who Look Like Me To Tell Me:

What I Love About My Skin Today: I Will Not Allow Others Who Do Not Look Like Me To Tell Me:

I Am Proud To Be: It Is Okay If I Am The Only One:

I Am Beautiful/Good Looking Because: It Is Okay If I Do Not Fit Into:

The Last Negative Comment I Received Towards My Appearance/Personality And My Thoughts Towards The Comment: Everyday I Am Learning To Accept:

How Did I Respond Towards The Comment Made In The Previous Prompt?   Just Because I Don't/Do _____, Doesn't Mean I:

It Is Okay For Me To Like

_____

And Still Be:

Loving Me For Who I Am

Date: Mood:

What I Love About My Hair Today: I Will Not Allow Others Who Look Like Me To Tell Me:

What I Love About My Skin Today: I Will Not Allow Others Who Do Not Look Like Me To Tell Me:

I Am Proud To Be: It Is Okay If I Am The Only One:

I Am Beautiful/Good Looking Because: It Is Okay If I Do Not Fit Into:

The Last Negative Comment I Received Towards My Appearance/Personality And My Thoughts Towards The Comment: Everyday I Am Learning To Accept:

How Did I Respond Towards The Comment Made In The Previous Prompt?   Just Because I Don't/Do

_____, Doesn't Mean I:

It Is Okay For Me To Like
_____
And Still Be:

I Know That I Am Fearless And Fabulous Just As I Am.

Why Do I Think This Way? Why Do They Think This Way?
— The Truth

The People Need Healing.

Loving Me For Who I Am

Date: Mood:

What I Love About My Hair Today: I Will Not Allow Others Who Look Like Me To Tell Me:

What I Love About My Skin Today: I Will Not Allow Others Who Do Not Look Like Me To Tell Me:

I Am Proud To Be: It Is Okay If I Am The Only One:

I Am Beautiful/Good Looking Because: It Is Okay If I Do Not Fit Into:

The Last Negative Comment I Received Towards My Appearance/Personality And My Thoughts Towards The Comment: Everyday I Am Learning To Accept:

How Did I Respond Towards The Comment Made In The Previous Prompt?   Just Because I Don't/Do

_____, Doesn't Mean I:

It Is Okay For Me To Like

_____

And Still Be:

I Have Faith In My Skills And In My Ability To Succeed And Get What I Want.

Loving Me For Who I Am

Date: Mood:

What I Love About My Hair Today: | I Will Not Allow Others Who Look Like Me To Tell Me:

What I Love About My Skin Today: | I Will Not Allow Others Who Do Not Look Like Me To Tell Me:

I Am Proud To Be: | It Is Okay If I Am The Only One:

I Am Beautiful/Good Looking Because: | It Is Okay If I Do Not Fit Into:

The Last Negative Comment I Received Towards My Appearance/Personality And My Thoughts Towards The Comment: | Everyday I Am Learning To Accept:

How Did I Respond Towards The Comment Made In The Previous Prompt? | Just Because I Don't/Do _____, Doesn't Mean I:

It Is Okay For Me To Like
_____
And Still Be:

I Am Inspired By Others Who Look Just Like Me. I Am Empowered To Go After My Goals Just Like Them.

Loving Me For Who I Am

Date: Mood:

What I Love About My Hair Today: I Will Not Allow Others Who Look Like Me To Tell Me:

What I Love About My Skin Today: I Will Not Allow Others Who Do Not Look Like Me To Tell Me:

I Am Proud To Be: It Is Okay If I Am The Only One:

I Am Beautiful/Good Looking Because: It Is Okay If I Do Not Fit Into:

The Last Negative Comment I Received Towards My Appearance/Personality And My Thoughts Towards The Comment: Everyday I Am Learning To Accept:

How Did I Respond Towards The Comment Made In The Previous Prompt?   Just Because I Don't/Do

_____, Doesn't Mean I:

It Is Okay For Me To Like
_____
And Still Be:

No One Is Better Than Me Because Of How They Look (Or For Any Other Reason).

How Has My Thoughts And Attitude About Skin Color Come Through In My Words And Actions?

Loving Me For Who I Am

Date: Mood:

What I Love About My Hair Today: I Will Not Allow Others Who Look Like Me To Tell Me:

What I Love About My Skin Today: I Will Not Allow Others Who Do Not Look Like Me To Tell Me:

I Am Proud To Be: It Is Okay If I Am The Only One:

I Am Beautiful/Good Looking Because: It Is Okay If I Do Not Fit Into:

The Last Negative Comment I Received Towards My Appearance/Personality And My Thoughts Towards The Comment: Everyday I Am Learning To Accept:

How Did I Respond Towards The Comment Made In The Previous Prompt?   Just Because I Don't/Do _____, Doesn't Mean I:

It Is Okay For Me To Like _____

And Still Be:

I Determine What Is Beautiful For Me Instead Of Relying On Other People's Perceptions.

Loving Me For Who I Am

Date: Mood:

What I Love About My Hair Today: | I Will Not Allow Others Who Look Like Me To Tell Me:

What I Love About My Skin Today: | I Will Not Allow Others Who Do Not Look Like Me To Tell Me:

I Am Proud To Be: | It Is Okay If I Am The Only One:

I Am Beautiful/Good Looking Because: | It Is Okay If I Do Not Fit Into:

The Last Negative Comment I Received Towards My Appearance/Personality And My Thoughts Towards The Comment: | Everyday I Am Learning To Accept:

How Did I Respond Towards The Comment Made In The Previous Prompt? | Just Because I Don't/Do

_____, Doesn't Mean I:

It Is Okay For Me To Like

_____

And Still Be:

The Way The World Treats Me Is Not Always Kind But The Way I Treat Myself Is Gentle And With Love.

Loving Me For Who I Am

Date: Mood:

What I Love About My Hair Today: I Will Not Allow Others Who Look Like Me To Tell Me:

What I Love About My Skin Today: I Will Not Allow Others Who Do Not Look Like Me To Tell Me:

I Am Proud To Be: It Is Okay If I Am The Only One:

I Am Beautiful/Good Looking Because: It Is Okay If I Do Not Fit Into:

The Last Negative Comment I Received Towards My Appearance/Personality And My Thoughts Towards The Comment: Everyday I Am Learning To Accept:

How Did I Respond Towards The Comment Made In The Previous Prompt?   Just Because I Don't/Do

_____, Doesn't Mean I:

It Is Okay For Me To Like

_____

And Still Be:

Accepting How I Look Is Part Of My Journey To Self-Love And Self-Confidence.

209

Loving Me For Who I Am

Date: Mood:

What I Love About My Hair Today:

I Will Not Allow Others Who Look Like Me To Tell Me:

What I Love About My Skin Today:

I Will Not Allow Others Who Do Not Look Like Me To Tell Me:

I Am Proud To Be:

It Is Okay If I Am The Only One:

I Am Beautiful/Good Looking Because:

It Is Okay If I Do Not Fit Into:

The Last Negative Comment I Received Towards My Appearance/Personality And My Thoughts Towards The Comment:

Everyday I Am Learning To Accept:

How Did I Respond Towards The Comment Made In The Previous Prompt?

Just Because I Don't/Do

_____, Doesn't Mean I:

It Is Okay For Me To Like _____ And Still Be:

Loving Me For Who I Am

Date: Mood:

What I Love About My Hair Today: I Will Not Allow Others Who Look Like Me To Tell Me:

What I Love About My Skin Today: I Will Not Allow Others Who Do Not Look Like Me To Tell Me:

I Am Proud To Be: It Is Okay If I Am The Only One:

I Am Beautiful/Good Looking Because: It Is Okay If I Do Not Fit Into:

The Last Negative Comment I Received Towards My Appearance/Personality And My Thoughts Towards The Comment: Everyday I Am Learning To Accept:

How Did I Respond Towards The Comment Made In The Previous Prompt?   Just Because I Don't/Do

_____, Doesn't Mean I:

It Is Okay For Me To Like

_____

And Still Be:

Since I Started Embracing My Heritage, My Newfound Confidence Is Radiating From Within Me.

I Will No Longer Allow Anyone To Punish Me Because Of My Skin.

Loving Me For Who I Am

Date:					Mood:

What I Love About My Hair Today:

I Will Not Allow Others Who Look Like Me To Tell Me:

What I Love About My Skin Today:

I Will Not Allow Others Who Do Not Look Like Me To Tell Me:

I Am Proud To Be:

It Is Okay If I Am The Only One:

I Am Beautiful/Good Looking Because:

It Is Okay If I Do Not Fit Into:

The Last Negative Comment I Received Towards My Appearance/Personality And My Thoughts Towards The Comment:

Everyday I Am Learning To Accept:

How Did I Respond Towards The Comment Made In The Previous Prompt?

Just Because I Don't/Do

_____, Doesn't Mean I:

It Is Okay For Me To Like

_____

And Still Be:

I Hold My Head Up High As I Walk Among Crowds Of Different Looking People.

Loving Me For Who I Am

Date: Mood:

What I Love About My Hair Today: I Will Not Allow Others Who Look Like
                                                   Me To Tell Me:

What I Love About My Skin Today: I Will Not Allow Others Who Do Not
                                                   Look Like Me To Tell Me:

I Am Proud To Be: It Is Okay If I Am The Only One:

I Am Beautiful/Good Looking   It Is Okay If I Do Not Fit Into:
Because:

The Last Negative Comment I   Everyday I Am Learning To Accept:
Received Towards My Appearance/
Personality And My Thoughts
Towards The Comment:

How Did I Respond Towards The   Just Because I Don't/Do
Comment Made In The Previous
Prompt?   _____, Doesn't Mean I:

It Is Okay For Me To Like
_____
And Still Be:

I Have Stopped Being Afraid Of Who I Am And That Makes Me Even More Beautiful!

214

Loving Me For Who I Am

Date: Mood:

What I Love About My Hair Today: I Will Not Allow Others Who Look Like Me To Tell Me:

What I Love About My Skin Today: I Will Not Allow Others Who Do Not Look Like Me To Tell Me:

I Am Proud To Be: It Is Okay If I Am The Only One:

I Am Beautiful/Good Looking Because: It Is Okay If I Do Not Fit Into:

The Last Negative Comment I Received Towards My Appearance/Personality And My Thoughts Towards The Comment: Everyday I Am Learning To Accept:

How Did I Respond Towards The Comment Made In The Previous Prompt?   Just Because I Don't/Do

_____, Doesn't Mean I:

It Is Okay For Me To Like
_____
And Still Be:

My Faith In God And Love For Myself Are The Two Things That Will Help Me Reach My Full Potential.

215

Every Shade Is Beautiful.

My Thoughts

Loving Me For Who I Am

Date: Mood:

What I Love About My Hair Today: I Will Not Allow Others Who Look Like Me To Tell Me:

What I Love About My Skin Today: I Will Not Allow Others Who Do Not Look Like Me To Tell Me:

I Am Proud To Be: It Is Okay If I Am The Only One:

I Am Beautiful/Good Looking Because: It Is Okay If I Do Not Fit Into:

The Last Negative Comment I Received Towards My Appearance/Personality And My Thoughts Towards The Comment: Everyday I Am Learning To Accept:

How Did I Respond Towards The Comment Made In The Previous Prompt?   Just Because I Don't/Do

_____, Doesn't Mean I:

It Is Okay For Me To Like

_____

And Still Be:

I Look And Sound Different From Everyone Around Me And I Am Perfectly Fine With That.

218

Loving Me For Who I Am

Date: Mood:

What I Love About My Hair Today: I Will Not Allow Others Who Look Like Me To Tell Me:

What I Love About My Skin Today: I Will Not Allow Others Who Do Not Look Like Me To Tell Me:

I Am Proud To Be: It Is Okay If I Am The Only One:

I Am Beautiful/Good Looking Because: It Is Okay If I Do Not Fit Into:

The Last Negative Comment I Received Towards My Appearance/Personality And My Thoughts Towards The Comment: Everyday I Am Learning To Accept:

How Did I Respond Towards The Comment Made In The Previous Prompt?   Just Because I Don't/Do

_____, Doesn't Mean I:

It Is Okay For Me To Like

_____

And Still Be:

I Make It A Point To Be A Role Model Against Colorism.

Loving Me For Who I Am

Date: Mood:

What I See In The Mirror Is What Matters.

What I Love About My Hair Today:

I Will Not Allow Others Who Look Like Me To Tell Me:

What I Love About My Skin Today:

I Will Not Allow Others Who Do Not Look Like Me To Tell Me:

I Am Proud To Be:

It Is Okay If I Am The Only One:

I Am Beautiful/Good Looking Because:

It Is Okay If I Do Not Fit Into:

The Last Negative Comment I Received Towards My Appearance/Personality And My Thoughts Towards The Comment:

Everyday I Am Learning To Accept:

How Did I Respond Towards The Comment Made In The Previous Prompt?

Just Because I Don't/Do

_____, Doesn't Mean I:

It Is Okay For Me To Like

_____

And Still Be:

I Will Not Take On Their Inferiority Complex.

I Found My Confidence And I Soared.

Loving Me For Who I Am

Date: Mood:

What I Love About My Hair Today: | I Will Not Allow Others Who Look Like Me To Tell Me:

What I Love About My Skin Today: | I Will Not Allow Others Who Do Not Look Like Me To Tell Me:

I Am Proud To Be: | It Is Okay If I Am The Only One:

I Am Beautiful/Good Looking Because: | It Is Okay If I Do Not Fit Into:

The Last Negative Comment I Received Towards My Appearance/Personality And My Thoughts Towards The Comment: | Everyday I Am Learning To Accept:

How Did I Respond Towards The Comment Made In The Previous Prompt? | Just Because I Don't/Do _____, Doesn't Mean I:

It Is Okay For Me To Like

_____

And Still Be:

My Dreams Are Valid Regardless Of What Anyone Says.

Loving Me For Who I Am

Date: Mood:

What I Love About My Hair Today: I Will Not Allow Others Who Look Like Me To Tell Me:

What I Love About My Skin Today: I Will Not Allow Others Who Do Not Look Like Me To Tell Me:

I Am Proud To Be: It Is Okay If I Am The Only One:

I Am Beautiful/Good Looking Because: It Is Okay If I Do Not Fit Into:

The Last Negative Comment I Received Towards My Appearance/Personality And My Thoughts Towards The Comment: Everyday I Am Learning To Accept:

How Did I Respond Towards The Comment Made In The Previous Prompt?   Just Because I Don't/Do

_____ _____, Doesn't Mean I:

It Is Okay For Me To Like

_____

And Still Be:

Loving Me For Who I Am

Date: Mood:

What I Love About My Hair Today: I Will Not Allow Others Who Look Like Me To Tell Me:

What I Love About My Skin Today: I Will Not Allow Others Who Do Not Look Like Me To Tell Me:

I Am Proud To Be: It Is Okay If I Am The Only One:

I Am Beautiful/Good Looking Because: It Is Okay If I Do Not Fit Into:

The Last Negative Comment I Received Towards My Appearance/Personality And My Thoughts Towards The Comment: Everyday I Am Learning To Accept:

How Did I Respond Towards The Comment Made In The Previous Prompt?   Just Because I Don't/Do

_____, Doesn't Mean I:

It Is Okay For Me To Like

_____

And Still Be:

I Am Focused On Improving My Life And Myself Inside And Out.

Do You Know How Beautiful You Are?

How Does My Thoughts And Attitude About Skin Color Change Things For Me Personally and With Others That I Encounter?

Loving Me For Who I Am

Date: Mood:

What I Love About My Hair Today:

I Will Not Allow Others Who Look Like Me To Tell Me:

What I Love About My Skin Today:

I Will Not Allow Others Who Do Not Look Like Me To Tell Me:

I Am Proud To Be:

It Is Okay If I Am The Only One:

I Am Beautiful/Good Looking Because:

It Is Okay If I Do Not Fit Into:

The Last Negative Comment I Received Towards My Appearance/Personality And My Thoughts Towards The Comment:

Everyday I Am Learning To Accept:

How Did I Respond Towards The Comment Made In The Previous Prompt?

Just Because I Don't/Do

_____, Doesn't Mean I:

It Is Okay For Me To Like

_____

And Still Be:

Loving Me For Who I Am

Date: Mood:

What I Love About My Hair Today: I Will Not Allow Others Who Look Like
                                         Me To Tell Me:

What I Love About My Skin Today: I Will Not Allow Others Who Do Not
                                         Look Like Me To Tell Me:

I Am Proud To Be: It Is Okay If I Am The Only One:

I Am Beautiful/Good Looking   It Is Okay If I Do Not Fit Into:
Because:

The Last Negative Comment I   Everyday I Am Learning To Accept:
Received Towards My Appearance/
Personality And My Thoughts
Towards The Comment:

How Did I Respond Towards The   Just Because I Don't/Do
Comment Made In The Previous
Prompt?   _____, Doesn't Mean I:

It Is Okay For Me To Like

_____

And Still Be:

It Does Not Matter How The World Treats Me When I Know The Only Thing That Matters Is The Way I Treat Myself.

Loving Me For Who I Am

Date: Mood:

What I Love About My Hair Today: I Will Not Allow Others Who Look Like Me To Tell Me:

What I Love About My Skin Today: I Will Not Allow Others Who Do Not Look Like Me To Tell Me:

I Am Proud To Be: It Is Okay If I Am The Only One:

I Am Beautiful/Good Looking Because: It Is Okay If I Do Not Fit Into:

The Last Negative Comment I Received Towards My Appearance/Personality And My Thoughts Towards The Comment: Everyday I Am Learning To Accept:

How Did I Respond Towards The Comment Made In The Previous Prompt?   Just Because I Don't/Do

_____ _____, Doesn't Mean I:

It Is Okay For Me To Like

_____

And Still Be:

I Will Not Allow How The World Likes To View Me To Stop Me From Achieving What I Dreamed Of And Deserve.

230

Anyone Who Looks Like Me Is Just As Beautiful And I Will Always Show Them Love.

There Are Special Hearts And Eyes That Defy Society's Stereotypes And See Me For The Beauty That I AM.

Loving Me For Who I Am

Date: Mood:

What I Love About My Hair Today: I Will Not Allow Others Who Look Like Me To Tell Me:

What I Love About My Skin Today: I Will Not Allow Others Who Do Not Look Like Me To Tell Me:

I Am Proud To Be: It Is Okay If I Am The Only One:

I Am Beautiful/Good Looking Because: It Is Okay If I Do Not Fit Into:

The Last Negative Comment I Received Towards My Appearance/Personality And My Thoughts Towards The Comment: Everyday I Am Learning To Accept:

How Did I Respond Towards The Comment Made In The Previous Prompt?   Just Because I Don't/Do

_____, Doesn't Mean I:

It Is Okay For Me To Like

_____

And Still Be:

Love Doesn't Put Down How I Look.

233

Loving Me For Who I Am

Date: Mood:

What I Love About My Hair Today:

I Will Not Allow Others Who Look Like Me To Tell Me:

What I Love About My Skin Today:

I Will Not Allow Others Who Do Not Look Like Me To Tell Me:

I Am Proud To Be:

It Is Okay If I Am The Only One:

I Am Beautiful/Good Looking Because:

It Is Okay If I Do Not Fit Into:

The Last Negative Comment I Received Towards My Appearance/Personality And My Thoughts Towards The Comment:

Everyday I Am Learning To Accept:

How Did I Respond Towards The Comment Made In The Previous Prompt?

Just Because I Don't/Do

_____ _____, Doesn't Mean I:

It Is Okay For Me To Like
_____
And Still Be:

Loving Me For Who I Am

Date: Mood:

What I Love About My Hair Today: I Will Not Allow Others Who Look Like Me To Tell Me:

What I Love About My Skin Today: I Will Not Allow Others Who Do Not Look Like Me To Tell Me:

I Am Proud To Be: It Is Okay If I Am The Only One:

I Am Beautiful/Good Looking Because: It Is Okay If I Do Not Fit Into:

The Last Negative Comment I Received Towards My Appearance/Personality And My Thoughts Towards The Comment: Everyday I Am Learning To Accept:

How Did I Respond Towards The Comment Made In The Previous Prompt?   Just Because I Don't/Do

_____, Doesn't Mean I:

It Is Okay For Me To Like

_____

And Still Be:

Being Comfortable And Confident In My Own Skin Is Definitely Worth It.

My Thoughts

How Do I Feel About The Opposite Sex Who Have The Same Skin Complexion As Me?

Am I Attracted To Those Of The Opposite Sex That Are Lighter Or Darker Than Me? Why Or Why Not?

Loving Me For Who I Am

Date: Mood:

What I Love About My Hair Today: I Will Not Allow Others Who Look Like Me To Tell Me:

What I Love About My Skin Today: I Will Not Allow Others Who Do Not Look Like Me To Tell Me:

I Am Proud To Be: It Is Okay If I Am The Only One:

I Am Beautiful/Good Looking Because: It Is Okay If I Do Not Fit Into:

The Last Negative Comment I Received Towards My Appearance/Personality And My Thoughts Towards The Comment: Everyday I Am Learning To Accept:

How Did I Respond Towards The Comment Made In The Previous Prompt?   Just Because I Don't/Do

_____ _____, Doesn't Mean I:

It Is Okay For Me To Like

_____

And Still Be:

I Live In My Truth Each Day By Being True To Who I Am.

238

Loving Me For Who I Am

Date: Mood:

What I Love About My Hair Today: I Will Not Allow Others Who Look Like Me To Tell Me:

What I Love About My Skin Today: I Will Not Allow Others Who Do Not Look Like Me To Tell Me:

I Am Proud To Be: It Is Okay If I Am The Only One:

I Am Beautiful/Good Looking Because: It Is Okay If I Do Not Fit Into:

The Last Negative Comment I Received Towards My Appearance/Personality And My Thoughts Towards The Comment: Everyday I Am Learning To Accept:

How Did I Respond Towards The Comment Made In The Previous Prompt?   Just Because I Don't/Do

_____, Doesn't Mean I:

It Is Okay For Me To Like

_____

And Still Be:

I Celebrate Others Who Look Like Me As Well. I Know We Are All Beautiful.

Loving Me For Who I Am

Date: Mood:

What I Love About My Hair Today: I Will Not Allow Others Who Look Like Me To Tell Me:

What I Love About My Skin Today: I Will Not Allow Others Who Do Not Look Like Me To Tell Me:

I Am Proud To Be: It Is Okay If I Am The Only One:

I Am Beautiful/Good Looking Because: It Is Okay If I Do Not Fit Into:

The Last Negative Comment I Received Towards My Appearance/Personality And My Thoughts Towards The Comment: Everyday I Am Learning To Accept:

How Did I Respond Towards The Comment Made In The Previous Prompt?   Just Because I Don't/Do

_____ _____, Doesn't Mean I:

It Is Okay For Me To Like

_____

And Still Be:

Every Day, I Consciously Cultivate Self-Love Practices And Steer Away From Negative Self-Talk.

My Thoughts

Some Of My Experiences Have Brought Me To Tears, But Moving Forward I Will Shine.

Loving Me For Who I Am

Date: Mood:

What I Love About My Hair Today: I Will Not Allow Others Who Look Like Me To Tell Me:

What I Love About My Skin Today: I Will Not Allow Others Who Do Not Look Like Me To Tell Me:

I Am Proud To Be: It Is Okay If I Am The Only One:

I Am Beautiful/Good Looking Because: It Is Okay If I Do Not Fit Into:

The Last Negative Comment I Received Towards My Appearance/Personality And My Thoughts Towards The Comment: Everyday I Am Learning To Accept:

How Did I Respond Towards The Comment Made In The Previous Prompt?   Just Because I Don't/Do

_____, Doesn't Mean I:

It Is Okay For Me To Like

_____

And Still Be:

I Am A Beautiful Being Because I Truly Love And Accept Myself.

243

Loving Me For Who I Am

Date: Mood:

What I Love About My Hair Today: I Will Not Allow Others Who Look Like Me To Tell Me:

What I Love About My Skin Today: I Will Not Allow Others Who Do Not Look Like Me To Tell Me:

I Am Proud To Be: It Is Okay If I Am The Only One:

I Am Beautiful/Good Looking Because: It Is Okay If I Do Not Fit Into:

The Last Negative Comment I Received Towards My Appearance/Personality And My Thoughts Towards The Comment: Everyday I Am Learning To Accept:

How Did I Respond Towards The Comment Made In The Previous Prompt?   Just Because I Don't/Do

__ _____, Doesn't Mean I:

It Is Okay For Me To Like
_____
And Still Be:

Thank You, Thank You, Thank You God For Creating Me Just As I Am.

244

Loving Me For Who I Am

Date: Mood:

What I Love About My Hair Today: | I Will Not Allow Others Who Look Like Me To Tell Me:

What I Love About My Skin Today: | I Will Not Allow Others Who Do Not Look Like Me To Tell Me:

I Am Proud To Be: | It Is Okay If I Am The Only One:

I Am Beautiful/Good Looking Because: | It Is Okay If I Do Not Fit Into:

The Last Negative Comment I Received Towards My Appearance/Personality And My Thoughts Towards The Comment: | Everyday I Am Learning To Accept:

How Did I Respond Towards The Comment Made In The Previous Prompt? | Just Because I Don't/Do _____, Doesn't Mean I:

It Is Okay For Me To Like _____ And Still Be:

It Is Becoming Easier And Easier For Me To See The Beauty In Myself.

245

How Do I Feel About Having Friends/Children Who Look And/Or Talk Like Me?

My Thoughts

Loving Me For Who I Am

Date: Mood:

What I Love About My Hair Today:

I Will Not Allow Others Who Look Like Me To Tell Me:

What I Love About My Skin Today:

I Will Not Allow Others Who Do Not Look Like Me To Tell Me:

I Am Proud To Be:

It Is Okay If I Am The Only One:

I Am Beautiful/Good Looking Because:

It Is Okay If I Do Not Fit Into:

The Last Negative Comment I Received Towards My Appearance/Personality And My Thoughts Towards The Comment:

Everyday I Am Learning To Accept:

How Did I Respond Towards The Comment Made In The Previous Prompt?

Just Because I Don't/Do _____, Doesn't Mean I:

It Is Okay For Me To Like _____ And Still Be:

I Am Not Pretty/Good Looking For Anything. I Am Just Pretty/Good Looking.

Loving Me For Who I Am

Date: Mood:

What I Love About My Hair Today: I Will Not Allow Others Who Look Like Me To Tell Me:

What I Love About My Skin Today: I Will Not Allow Others Who Do Not Look Like Me To Tell Me:

I Am Proud To Be: It Is Okay If I Am The Only One:

I Am Beautiful/Good Looking Because: It Is Okay If I Do Not Fit Into:

The Last Negative Comment I Received Towards My Appearance/Personality And My Thoughts Towards The Comment: Everyday I Am Learning To Accept:

How Did I Respond Towards The Comment Made In The Previous Prompt?   Just Because I Don't/Do

_____, Doesn't Mean I:

It Is Okay For Me To Like
_____
And Still Be:

The Right People Love Me For Who I Am.

Loving Me For Who I Am

Date: Mood:

What I Love About My Hair Today: I Will Not Allow Others Who Look Like Me To Tell Me:

What I Love About My Skin Today: I Will Not Allow Others Who Do Not Look Like Me To Tell Me:

I Am Proud To Be: It Is Okay If I Am The Only One:

I Am Beautiful/Good Looking Because: It Is Okay If I Do Not Fit Into:

The Last Negative Comment I Received Towards My Appearance/Personality And My Thoughts Towards The Comment:

Everyday I Am Learning To Accept:

How Did I Respond Towards The Comment Made In The Previous Prompt?

Just Because I Don't/Do _____, Doesn't Mean I:

It Is Okay For Me To Like _____

And Still Be:

Other People's Perception Of Beauty Will Not Change Who/What I Want In My Life And How I Treat Others.

250

My Thoughts

Loving Me For Who I Am

Date: Mood:

What I Love About My Hair Today: | I Will Not Allow Others Who Look Like
                                         | Me To Tell Me:

What I Love About My Skin Today: | I Will Not Allow Others Who Do Not
                                         | Look Like Me To Tell Me:

I Am Proud To Be: | It Is Okay If I Am The Only One:

I Am Beautiful/Good Looking | It Is Okay If I Do Not Fit Into:
Because:

The Last Negative Comment I | Everyday I Am Learning To Accept:
Received Towards My Appearance/
Personality And My Thoughts
Towards The Comment:

How Did I Respond Towards The | Just Because I Don't/Do
Comment Made In The Previous
Prompt? | ____ _____, Doesn't Mean I:

It Is Okay For Me To Like
_____
And Still Be:

I Will Not Allow Other People's Preferences To Affect My Preferences.

Loving Me For Who I Am

Date: Mood:

What I Love About My Hair Today: I Will Not Allow Others Who Look Like Me To Tell Me:

What I Love About My Skin Today: I Will Not Allow Others Who Do Not Look Like Me To Tell Me:

I Am Proud To Be: It Is Okay If I Am The Only One:

I Am Beautiful/Good Looking Because: It Is Okay If I Do Not Fit Into:

The Last Negative Comment I Received Towards My Appearance/Personality And My Thoughts Towards The Comment: Everyday I Am Learning To Accept:

How Did I Respond Towards The Comment Made In The Previous Prompt?   Just Because I Don't/Do

_____, Doesn't Mean I:

It Is Okay For Me To Like

_____

And Still Be:

I Know My Worth. I Do Not Allow Others To Make Me Feel Worthless.

253

Loving Me For Who I Am

Date: Mood:

What I Love About My Hair Today: I Will Not Allow Others Who Look Like
                                                    Me To Tell Me:

What I Love About My Skin Today: I Will Not Allow Others Who Do Not
                                                    Look Like Me To Tell Me:

I Am Proud To Be: It Is Okay If I Am The Only One:

I Am Beautiful/Good Looking   It Is Okay If I Do Not Fit Into:
Because:

The Last Negative Comment I   Everyday I Am Learning To Accept:
Received Towards My Appearance/
Personality And My Thoughts
Towards The Comment:

How Did I Respond Towards The   Just Because I Don't/Do
Comment Made In The Previous
Prompt?   _____, Doesn't Mean I:

It Is Okay For Me To Like
_____
And Still Be:

I Am The Right Shade. I Have The Right Eyes. I Have The Right Smile. I Have The Right Nose. I Have The Right Lips. There Is Nothing Wrong With Me.

Made in the USA
Columbia, SC
09 February 2020

87658480R00152